Diaper Changes

The Complete Diapering Book
And Resource Guide

Diaper Changes

The Complete Diapering Book
And Resource Guide

3rd Edition

Theresa Rodriguez Farrisi

Foreword by
Janet Primomo, Ph.D., R.N.

M. Evans and Company, Inc.
New York

M. Evans and Company, Inc.
216 East 49th Street
New York, New York 10017
www.MEvans.com

Illustrations by Celia Mitchell—cmitchell@adelphia.net
The illustration of the Snappi used by permission of Baby Connections, Forest Hills, CA.
The illustration of the Diaper Duck used by permission of F&H Baby Products, Chagrin Falls, OH.
The illustration of the snap diaper and snap diaper cover used by permission of Motherease, Inc. Niagra Falls, NY.
Cover photography by Reddinger Photography, Myerstown, PA.
Cover and interior design by Rosewood Design, Richland, PA

Library of Congress Cataloging-in-Publication Data

Farrisi, Theresa Rodriguez, 1962–
    Diaper changes: the complete diapering book and resource guide / Theresa Rodriguez Farrisi; foreword by Janet Primomo—3rd ed.
        p.   cm.
    Includes bibliographic references and index.
    ISBN 1-59077-022-6
    1. Infants (Newborn)—Care. 2. Diapers. 3. Child Care. I. Title.
RJ61.F34 2003
649'.122—dc21   2002044769

Printed in the United States of America

9 8 7 6 5 4 3 2 1

To my mothers
And my children

CONTENTS

Diapering today is not what it used to be! • Making your life easier • What
you need, where to get it, how to use it • For new moms, cloth moms,
"maybe-cloth" moms • Full or part-timers welcome • Diapering facts and
issues you need to know • How to use this book • When you are done

Why it is a joy to relish natural fibers • The beautiful . . . drudgery? •
Dressed in plastic • Finding your own balance between cloth and disposables • What is convenience?

The olden days: flat (birdseye and gauze) • Prefolds: standard and diaper
service quality • Flannel/terry combinations • Alternative diapers: fitted and
contours • All-in-one diapers • Green and organic cotton • Hemp diapers
• Chinese and Egyptian cotton • Diaper doubler • My observations and recommendations

The olden days again: vinyl and pull-ons • Wool diaper covers: soakers and
Velcro styles • Cotton covers • Synthetic covers • On Velcro • Adult and
youth diapering • Recommendations

QUICK REFERENCE CHARTS:

Pins, clips, Snappis • Liners: throwaway and reusable • The diaper bucket
and bucket liners • Changing pads and bed pads • The Diaper Duck and
the diaper dip • Deodorizers • Changing tables • Ditty bags • On the diaper bag • Cleaning agents • The wipe warmer • Ointments and creams •
On baby wipes • Baby powders • The herbal difference • About training
pants • Swim diapers • Pottys

List of Illustrations

Foreword

It has been almost a decade since concerned nurses in the Seattle area began to question the health and environmental consequences of disposable diapers. Much to our surprise, there was virtually nothing on the potential environmental effects of disposable diapers in the professional literature. As a member of the King County Nurses Association in Seattle, I was involved in a series of projects aimed to provide parents and professionals with information about diapering alternatives and to influence policy on the issue. Our educational efforts were funded by local and state government as well as the U.S. Environmental Protection Agency. King County Nurses Association provided parents with information so that they could make informed choices about diapering and succeeded in raising awareness about diapering choices among professionals and policy makers.

Now, ten years later, Theresa Rodriguez Farrisi has moved beyond the work of King County Nurses Association to provide an extensive, indepth resource guide to assist parents in choosing diapering methods. *Diaper Changes* provides practical tips on the act of diapering not found in other books on parenting. In her book, Ms. Rodriguez Farrisi presents valuable information on the cost of diapering and complex environmental issues related to different diapering methods. Her book includes a thorough description of the various types of fabrics used in cloth diapers, new products to cover cloth diapers, laundering procedures, where to purchase products, and instruction on how to make diapers and covers.

Diaper Changes is an excellent resource for parents, childbirth educators, and health care providers. Ms. Rodriguez Farrisi suggests an approach to diapering that minimizes the use of chemicals and materials. Her book will assist others who share a concern for our environment in making sound choices about diapering products.

Janet Primomo, Ph.D., R.N.
University of Washington, Tacoma

INTRODUCTION

Why You Need This Book and How to Use It

Diapering today is not what it used to be!

What kind of diaper to use? Isn't cloth messy? How much money do I need to spend? What about the environment?

With all the changes which have transformed this basic parenting skill from obsolescence to state-of-the-art in recent years, there are indeed many questions to be raised about diapering today. I spent lots of money and an awful lot of time searching for the best possible diapering system, hoping to find solutions to the problems I encountered in using both cloth and disposable diapers. Would you believe that with six children (at times past with three in diapers—two full-time and one part-time) the statistics tell me that I have changed something like fifty thousand diapers! Through all of that I was looking at the *changes* in diapering over the past few years, making a lot of mental notes, remembering both the noteworthy and the unforgettably bad. (Mail order companies from coast to coast lust to get me on their mailing lists.)

Making your life easier

Through trial, error, determination, and now, through the writing of this book, I have gotten to know what they sell. I want you to know what I've found, and perhaps introduce you to some new things you haven't been aware of before.

Wouldn't you like to have someone learn all about it, make all the mistakes for you, saving you time, energy and money? That's what *Diaper Changes* is all about. Here, in one handy, informative book, is all the information you need about diapering. There has never been a book like this before in America.

1

DIAPER CHANGES

What you need, where to get it, how to use it

Diapers? Diaper covers? Diaper buckets? Wipes? Going out? Washing? It's all in here—different types, styles, and brands, quality, price, what's good and not so good. Plus, the second half of the book reviews all of the current mail order companies and the diapering products they sell, so you can really find what you are looking for. Or maybe something you weren't looking for, but glad you found!

For new moms, cloth moms, "maybe-cloth" moms

Are you a new mother or mother-to-be? Start here and you'll be set for the next two and a half years! *Are you considering how cloth might work for you?* Many companies offer great sample deals so you won't spend a lot of money finding out what you like or didn't like.

Have you used cloth before, but things didn't work out? Maybe it was the products you were using. Real advances have been made in construction, quality, and function in recent years. Disappointments like red marks, Velcro rubbing, or leakage are really a thing of the past. You will be amazed at what's out there, how satisfied you will be, and how eager these businesses are to see you succeed!

Full or part-timers welcome

Many parents—for environmental, health, cost, or aesthetic reasons—will never, ever use disposables—and I am on your side! But some will be happier using cloth part-time, and disposables part time—and I want you to feel at home here, too.

But am I a cloth purist? Pretty much. I must admit that I'm a lot "greener" now than I was when I started this book. You can't remain impartial after you've learned what's really going on in the disposable diapering world!

Diapering facts and issues you need to know

To help you also become fully informed about the "diaper debate," and save you a lot of time and energy, I review cost, environmental, and health considerations between disposables, diaper service, and home diapering. This way I do all the legwork for you and all you have to do is read!

Many of us came to motherhood having lost some of the old-timey knowledge of past generations, like how to breast-feed, make your own baby food, or use cloth diapers. Fortunately, we can all help each other regain ground and re-establish the continuum of past ages to now.

Diaper Changes is beautifully illustrated, so if you've got all of your samples, you can practice a bit before baby comes, or do some hands on learning with your little one at home. And for the frugal and/or creative, I offer suggestions and resources for making much of the stuff you need for diapering.

How to use this book

Chapters 1 to 10 deal with *everything you need to know about diapering*—different types of diapers, covers, and other products; how to diaper; laundry; going out and staying home; home diapering, diaper service, and disposables compared; costs; the environment; health and safety; and a make-your-own section.

In the back of the book is a *product index*, which you will find very useful for tracking down a certain type of diaper, diaper cover, alternative cleaning agent, or whatever you are looking for. Each category of product will have a list below it which tells you which companies sell that product.

The *Company and Resource Guide*, between these two sections of the book, is a handy review of approximately thirty highly reputable internet and mail-order companies from the U.S. and Canada which sell diapering products. You can read the entire guide, or merely under those companies you found in the product index had that specific something you are looking for.

Also included is a guide to youth and adult diapering products; sources for the environmental, cost, health, and safety information provided in this book; and a list of suppliers of sewing and fabric needs for those who would like to make their own diapering products.

I want you to enjoy this book, and enjoy diapering a whole lot more after you've found what products and diapering system work for you and your family.

When you are done

To mothers who might be trying cloth for the first time, especially after reading *Diaper Changes*, I want to thank you for letting me be a part of the process of trying something new. You'll get the hang of it quickly and be a pro in no time!

DIAPER CHANGES

To those of you who are looking for new cloth products after past failures, I believe you will find excellent products which can solve the problem or problems you've had in the past.

To new mothers, I want you to feel confident that the information provided in this book will enable you to make easy, confident diapering choices, and that this part of being a parent will be the least of your hassles!

Since I am one mother, with one set of likes and dislikes, you may find you love something I hate and hate something I love. That is wonderful! Even if you use disposables more than I do. Or really like to line dry and hand wash your diaper covers. Or you'd never use anything but your diaper service. The important thing is to use this book to find what works for you. And I know you will. You want what's best for your baby and your family.

Let's begin with a reflection on the art and practice of diapering.

CHAPTER 1

The Aesthetics of Diapering

Why it is a joy to relish natural fibers

The 1970s were a great decade for polyester. Do you remember those scratchy shirts with the big ties the guys wore? Or those shiny ladies' shirts? I guess people were eager for this man-made fabric because it wouldn't rip or tear easily. But it's so hot to wear a totally poly piece of clothing. It's sticky. It doesn't "breathe." So all your sweat and other forms of bodily moisture just hang around in the space between you and the fabric. You might as well wear a plastic bag!

Well, I suppose this is why people like natural fibers. Not because you look neatly ironed or plastically perfect, but because *it feels so good*. Many times I have enjoyed textiles, just stroking a nice piece of wool, or linen, or cotton. How about real, ancient silk velvet? Like other wholesome sensory pleasures, one can relish natural fabrics with abandon.

The beautiful . . . drudgery?

This is why I like cloth diapers. Almost entirely for the aesthetics of it. Certainly not because it is easier than plastic, but because it feels so good and looks so nice. (If you use a diaper service it really isn't much harder at all.) Those of you who live in the country understand the sense of ordered satisfaction of seeing a row of freshly-washed diapers hanging on a clothesline in the hot summer sun. The sweet way they smell after the air gets through them. A soft baby's butt and a soft diaper on it. This is the part I like best.

Then there's the part that isn't so nice. Rinsing that stinky diaper. Who can say that they love that? Or the way the diaper bucket can smell after a while. (I'll tell you about how to minimize that later. Procrastination in this area is definitely a habit to overcome!)

But sometimes a little drudgery is the price for greater aesthetic satisfaction. I guess in some sense the practice and art of diapering is a connection to cultures around the world and throughout time. This is really the way it's always been done, and the way most of the planet still does it. Everyone else manages to get by. Why can't we?

Dressed in plastic

And what about how a plastic diaper feels? I have some insight into this, because due to having nine and ten pound babies (I kid you not), I now experience chronic urinary incontinence—especially when pregnant. I have tried many things—old diapers (the contoured ones work great), Pampers (yes, I did), even the Attends. Boy, do those big plastic diapers for adults feel *gross*! Clammy and wet paperish mush rubbing on you! So how do you think your baby would like it? Some of you doubt your baby even notices. Okay, maybe not. But you do!

Finding your own balance between cloth and disposables

And here is my confession. My second daughter (who was trained at 2½) moves her little bowels two, three, four times *a day*. After both using a diaper service and doing my own almost exclusively for two years, I gave myself a break. (I also was diapering my under-one-year-old son at the same time and was played out from washing covers, too.) I used plastic on her exclusively for a few months until she trained. So I understand, therefore, if you want, like, or need to use disposables for any portion of your diapering experience!

Some people do end up making some kind of compromise. They might use cloth when at home (all the time), but put on plastic to go out. Or use cloth if it's a short, easy trip. Or disposables on airplanes and long journeys. Or during diarrhea or other illness. Or only if baby really wets a lot at night. Some cotton purists, however, bring their soft bundles with them *wherever*, and use a waterproof bag to bring it all home to wash or throw in the diaper service bucket. I was one of these for years! I brought a separate suitcase just for diapers when I visited my mother after my first child was born, and I traveled by airplane! I still do go out with my soft bundles and bring them home again, rather than use disposables, most of the time.

What is convenience?

It is here where personal judgment comes in to determine when and how much to use a convenience item. Can we use such items sparingly, and reusable items more often? If we saw disposables more this way it might help us decide how much we really need them, if ever.

Let's rethink the issue of convenience. It isn't so bad to throw a soiled diaper into a diaper bucket—no worse than throwing a disposable into the garbage. Diaper services are nearly as convenient as disposables—all you need to do is wash your diaper covers (and some services even do that for you). If you purchase your own diapers and home launder your time is well spent if it saves you enough money over time, say, to buy a real convenience item, like a dishwasher.

So, I encourage you to see how cloth diapering—whether home-laundered or with a service—will work for your family. No one should judge the decision you make, and how that decision changes as circumstances change. I only want to equip you to make the best possible decision for you and the ones you are privileged to care about.

The following two chapters detail all the new and different types of diapers, diaper covers, and accessories available today.

CHAPTER 2

Diapers—and What to Put over Them

A historical and cultural perspective

Have you ever wondered what people did in prior centuries to diaper their babies? Oh yes, we all remember those vinyl or "rubber" pants that were used with cloth diapers until about 1960 when Pampers forever changed the face of diapering. I've heard of Native American mothers using wads of peat moss inside their papooses. I guess they just reach in and grab whatever's in there and chuck it back on Mother Earth! The Amish we know keep both boys and girls in long dresses until they are two or so. Now I know why. They just stick a diaper on the baby, with no cover at all, and in theory, there's no clothing around the area to get wet! In Europe before the War the diapers were large and square and you folded them like a big kerchief and tied it on the baby in one big knot.

But can you imagine boiling diapers in a caldron, or scrubbing them out on rocks? What did they do in the days of the Industrial Revolution, when city folk just dumped their excrement onto the ever-burgeoning streets? Oh, people, we've got it easy! What's a little rinsing in the toilet, with indoor plumbing after all, and a load or two a week? Or letting a diaper service do virtually all the work for you? You don't even need the venerable clothesline anymore. (Ah, well. I still love the sight of diapers drying in the sun.)

So let's see what's come of diapering since the recent cloth renaissance and the development of many user-friendly products.

DIAPERS

The olden days: flat (birdseye and gauze)

The old-fashioned diapers were made of flour-sack material. In the old days flour came in soft cotton sacks that were converted into all manner of useful items, like dresses and diapers. The descendant of the flour sack diaper is the *flat* diaper, made of *gauze*—that soft, thin, quick-drying, loosely-woven fabric that some baby-boomers might remember their mothers using on them. *Birdseye* weave has little puckers in it and is more dense than gauze. It is used for other types of diapers as well.

flat gauze (folded)

Prefolds: standard and diaper service quality

Now we start getting more sophisticated. Somebody eventually thought up the idea to *prefold* the material so that it would be thicker, more absorbent, and require a little less work to get on baby. *Prefold* diapers basically come in two "weights"—the standard gauze or birdseye weight, which is found in any chain or children's store, and *diaper service quality*, a heavy, durable weight and thickness, available through the use of a diaper service or purchased through specialty mail-order. It is usually of twill—a dense, tight weave—with several absorbent inner layers. Some manufacturers, in an effort to make "regular" diapers heftier, put polyester fluff in the inner layers. (Why they do this is beyond me. Polyester does not absorb moisture.)

diaper service
quality prefold

Often diaper service or premium diapers have a terry cloth layer or layers either inside or on the outside of the diaper.

Prefolds are also made in all-flannel, birdseye, and green cotton or unbleached varieties. These are undoubtedly the most widely available type through any source.

Flannel/terry combinations

New on the horizon is a diaper of increasing popularity, which I have titled the *flannel/terry combo*. This diaper looks like a prefold, but it is only two layers—one piece of flannel (soft) and one piece of terrycloth (absorbent). Flannel/terry combos take less time to dry than regular prefolds, yet these two layers absorb as much moisture as other

**flannel/terry combo,
green cotton**

heavy-weight diapers. There is virtually no difference in folding these and folding prefolds—they
are about the same size. In reality if you diaper at
all you have to adjust one way or another, for size
of baby or whatever, so don't worry too much
about having to fold the diaper into the cover.

Alternative diapers: fitted and contours

As the interest in cloth diapering has
expanded, many "alternative" types of diapers
have made their advent. Because of the rise in popularity of diaper
covers as opposed to the old-fashioned plastic
(vinyl) pant, diapers have been consequently
designed to fit snugly inside the cover without
having to fold in the excess fabric. The idea is to
save yet another step in the diapering process.
These are the *contour* and the *fitted* diapers—
the contour being a kind of light bulb-shaped
thing and the fitted having elastic at the legs and
perhaps a Velcro or a snap closure which makes
them very snug on baby's
body. Pinnable contours

fitted snap diaper

**flannel/terry contour,
green cotton**

have an extra wing of material on either side
which makes them usable with pull-on covers.
Contour and fitted diapers come in flannel, flan-
nel/terry, knit terry, birdseye, gauze, and several
variations of shapes and styles.

All-in-one diapers

Eventually someone took the bother of a two-piece system out and
put the convenience of a disposable in. The *all-in-one* is a type constructed from a soft, inner layer, several
absorbent middle layers, elasticized legs
(much like fitted diapers) and a waterproof outer layer. The idea is to change
a cloth diaper like you would a disposable—take off, put on, no folds or fuss.
Almost all brands of all-in-ones have
Velcro closure, but some have snaps.

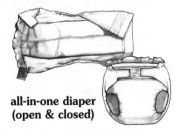

**all-in-one diaper
(open & closed)**

Green and organic cotton

The latest phenomenon on the diapering scene is the *green cotton* variety. This refers to the process of manufacturing which leaves out what many consider to be unnecessary and harmful things like bleaches, dyes, formaldehyde, and other pollutants, which are unhealthy both to human beings and the planet. The result is not a diaper which is green, but an off-white, creamy, oatmeal-beige color. This very, very soft textile is made into any type or style of diaper.

Organic green cotton is for the purest of the purest of the purest! Not only is the fabric untreated and unbleached, but the cotton itself is grown without chemical fertilizers, pesticides, herbicides, or defoliants. (The weeding is even done by hand!) The price tends to be high, but this is because of the special procedures involved to produce

green (unbleached)
birdseye prefold

it. (Production runs are also shorter, which make costs higher.) Still, this is the next wave in the environmental evolution of industry (along with the elimination of chlorine in paper manufacturing), so expect costs to drop as consumer interest increases.

The nice thing about green and organic cotton is that fecal stains tend to be brownish anyway, and you really stop worrying about diaper whiteness using them. They just kind of blend in to the color and don't show up much.

There is also a growing demand for organic cotton clothing, especially layette wear, where many parents would like something extremely soft and extremely pure next to their newborn's skin.

Chinese and Egyptian cotton

Diaper service diapers from China have been extremely popular, as they have traditionally been softer, more durable, and better made overall than many American counterparts. However, due to current restrictive trade quotas, most diaper service diapers are being obtained from other Asian countries and from Europe as of this writing, making the issue of "Chinese" diapers rather a non-issue. Egyptian cotton diapers have faced a similar predicament for several years.

Hemp diapers

Hemp is an ancient textile that used be used a great deal in boating (to make ropes for ships) because of its strength, mildew-resistance and ability to absorb/stay strong in water. Recently attemps have been made to make a diaper from hemp and cotton blends. Results? Mixed: some are scratcy and remind me of burlap, and others are just the softest and lovliest diaper on earth, more like fine, non-itchy wool than cotton. This is something whose day has truly yet to come.

Diaper doubler

Most companies offer a *diaper doubler*, which is a rectangular piece of coordinating diaper material providing absorbency without the bulk of an extra diaper.

green cotton diaper doubler

My observations and recommendations

I do not recommend the inexpensive, grocery store kind of prefold, especially if you plan to use pins or clips. (These are the small gauze prefold diapers, often with a polyester center padding.) Although diaper service quality or any of the flannel-type diapers tend to run about twice the price of the inferior quality ones (or more), the higher quality diapers are about three times as absorbent, and *extremely* durable. Many are made to be used by diaper services who wash them rigorously and re-use them endlessly. If you were to lay a regular-type, grocery-store prefold diaper next to one of the diaper service quality diapers you would immediately see the difference I am talking about. In this case, you are definitely getting what you pay for.

Flannel, however, is somewhat less durable than twill in the long run, especially if bleached. A few companies carry a heavy-duty flat flannel diaper which I would recommend if you like to fold them a certain way.

The contoured diapers can save a step in getting the diaper on the baby. Some are thick in the middle but very thin around the periphery, while others (like two-layer flannel/terry combos) are evenly thick throughout. You should sample two or three different styles to find one

with an absorbency level which meets your needs, as quality varies so immensely between manufacturers. Contour diapers do, however, make the best menstrual pads!

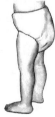

New products such as fitted diapers, snug covers, and all-in-ones make the old "soggy diaper look" obsolete!

Fitted diapers are nice if you want to use pull-on pants because they are snug and the ones with Velcro eliminate the need for fasteners of any kind. This system works well with newborn, breast-fed, runny, oozy poop. Some systems use both a fitted Velcro diaper and a Velcro diaper cover.

All-in-one diapers cost more per diaper than any combination out there. If you use a diaper liner, either reusable or throwaway, it will be easier to soak them (see chapter 3 about these). Most brands can be washed easily on hot and dried in the dryer, although some take two to three times longer to dry than even diaper service diapers (which are heavy to begin with). These are the costs of convenience, however, which I do feel are worth it! They are very easy to use. And other than using a diaper service, a one-piece system is the easiest way to go.

DIAPER COVERS, SOAKERS, PANTS

The olden days again: vinyl and pull-ons

In those olden days we spoke of before, the only way to diaper a baby was with a thin, flat diaper and "rubber" pants. (In the very olden days there were such things as nappies or soakers made from wool, likely fleeced, carded, spun, and knit on the family homestead from the family sheep.) These pants were and remain the vinyl packs of three which all the grocery and chain stores (unfortunately) carry.

The drawback is that when you use pull-ons you have to totally undress the bottom half of your baby in order to *slide* the diaper (poop and all) down the legs and off. Sometimes it does get on clothing or skin and is a real pain if your child has socks and shoes on! Then, of course, as disposables took the place of cloth we all became used to (and happy with) diapers which could simply fold up and fasten.

pull-on nylon pant

The first true diaper "covers" were like a disposable, sort of: they snapped across the front in two panels. With the subsequent arrival of Velcro for diapering one could diaper a baby without pins, get a good fit, and it had the feel of a disposable diaper change at long last.

So the dilemma today is finding the right combination of cover and diaper, choice of all-in-one, or simply type of cover, if you are using a diaper service. This is based on price, type desired, durability, ease of use, washability, features such as leg bindings or gussets, waterproofability, and "breathability."

Wool diaper covers: soakers and Velcro styles

Oh, how I love these. Soft, warm, cool in summer, nice to the touch. Lovely. These are made from a cream-colored wool felt, or for soakers—which are basically a pair of pull-on woolen underpants—a stretchy wool knit. Believe it or not, these really keep wetness in, because the lanolin in the wool maintains a kind of oily, water-resistant barrier. Wool also absorbs up to one third of its own weight in moisture without feeling wet. Because the fibers are kinky, they trap air and thus insulate. It is also ideal for diaper rash because wool is the most breathable fiber around—it stays several degrees cooler than any disposable similarly wrapped around baby. Wool fibers also do not promote bacterial growth—a plus for rashes.

wool knit soaker

Because of the use of animal fiber and the care involved in making them, wool covers are the most expensive diaper cover out there. All-in-ones, however, would average out to be higher in cost overall, but in both of these cases, I do feel you are getting what you pay for. And this has to be looked at in the context of spending two thousand dollars or more for disposables in your total diapering period to a few hundred dollars for all your cloth diapering products. Overall, you will spend hundreds and hundreds less than disposables, no matter which system or combination you end up using! And many of the better-made covers can be used for more than one baby. You may find you even like to use them with your diaper service.

Some mothers use wool at night (when they'd like something breathable for the long haul) and some other form of cover during the day. Others do just the opposite—they use wool during the day and a poly cover at

wool Velcro diaper cover

night, with a double diaper. This would be useful for heavy wetters who might eventually soak through the wool during a ten-hour sleep, although some claim they can go through the whole night in wool with no leaks! Some might use wool at night anyway and just change baby before a night nursing (when they are up anyway).

These covers really aren't a big hassle; it's a matter of how much you like wool, need breathability, prefer natural fibers, whatever. Whichever system you ultimately decide upon, with whichever type cover and diaper, will become your routine and you will get used to it.

Cotton covers

These come in an interesting array of styles and textile combinations. Some are either all-cotton, or a cotton blend, on the outside of the cover, with some kind of synthetic waterproofing bonded or sewn to the outer fabric as the inner "layer." Having cotton on the outside is mainly for the feel, but several companies do offer a specially-treated, all-cotton cover, inside and out. This is for true cotton purists, who really hate synthetic fibers!

I must admit to you, however, that once you start using something other than wool it's all about the same. A piece of fabric covered by something to keep baby's waste matter where it belongs—inside the diaper.

The main feature of a diaper should be absorbability; the main feature of a cover, beyond personal preference, should be waterproofability. Specially-treated all-cotton covers are tricky in terms of keeping waterproofability. Harsh detergents can wear this treatment right off. Check with the company or manufacturer as to which detergents are safe. Some companies are more honestly calling wool and cotton covers water-*resistant* rather than water*proof*.

A word here

No cover will stay waterproof indefinitely. None of them, not even the synthetic covers, is made from silicone or a garbage bag; wetness does eventually get through if you reach the saturation point. This is the real difference between a baby in plastic and a baby in cloth: you do need to change cloth more often. Usually, unless you get poop on it (and sometimes if it's not too bad you can just wipe it off), you need to change a cover for every three or so diaper changes. Some companies recommend rotating covers if they start to get moist by airing them out to dry off and use again before washing. This will also help covers wear better and last longer.

Synthetic Covers

There are five basic *man-made* or *synthetic* textiles used, and they vary immensely in terms of quality as well as construction. These are *polyester* (including Gore-Tex), *nylon, polyurethane,* and *vinyl.* New to the market in recent years is *microfleece* (or PolarFleece), such as is used in outerwear and sleepwear.

Poly knit covers are very durable. These often have a double poly layer, or an outer fabric layer like terry or nylon taffeta. These can take the dryer and non-chlorine bleaches. Hearty is the word! Gore-Tex is a breathable poly constructed in such a way as to allow water vapor to get out (keeping baby cool) but prevent water drops from doing the

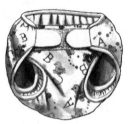

same (keeping clothes dry). This is the same fabric used in adult outerwear and sports shoes. Ultrex is another Gore-Tex type fabric with the same properties.

Nylon covers are also popular, for several reasons. They are about the cheapest kind to buy, of either the pull-on or Velcro kind. It is usually a soft, waterproofed, nylon taffeta. They are leagues above similar vinyl covers of any kind.

Velcro diaper cover

I have found, however, that coated nylon covers require more diligent special handling than most. They can be machine washed, but you have to avoid any detergent containing bleach, Borax, brighteners, or grease-releasers. These will strip off the waterproof coating and render them useless. Many folks just wash them by hand

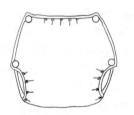

with mild dish soap and line dry. I have found this an unnecessary hassle when there are other good quality covers of other fabric combinations that do not require such kid glove handling.

Polyurethane covers work as well as the polyester covers in terms of ease of washing, drying, durability, and quality. Polyurethane is an inner coating, slick and smooth, usually

snap diaper cover

bonded to an outside layer of polyester or perhaps a cotton/poly blend. Any fecal matter which gets on it just slides off as you rinse it. They are worth the money you will spend.

Cloth Diaper Features

- **quickest drying:** all flat diapers, but gauze especially
- **softest:** fine knit terry; birdseye; certain flannels; green and organic cotton varieties, some hemp blend varieties
- **sturdiest:** diaper service quality prefolds
- **best fitting:** fitted Velcro or snap diapers; some all-in-ones
- **most absorbent:** any diaper with terry or hemp
- **easiest to use:** your diaper service; all-in-ones
- **most environmentally friendly:** your diaper service; organic and green cotton diapers
- **not recommended:** diapers with inner polyester fluff layer; synthetic diapers

PolarFleece and *microfleece* are wondrously lovely synthetic cousins of wool. These soft, waterproof, breathable fabrics are terrific for diaper covers. Fleece has come into vogue for use as diaper liners as well, because it is supposed to "wick the moisture" away from baby; but I have found that the liner is still moist after use and might not add up to a whole lot of difference from a diaper, plain cloth liner or good disposable liner (and can possibly retain heat next to the skin in hot or humid weather conditions). Fleece is absolutely terrific, however, over the diaper as a synthetic substitute for wool!.

Vinyl seems durable at first, but it eventually cracks (especially at stress points) and is easily warped by heat. It is also sticky, uncomfortable, and totally unbreathable, like plastic disposables. This is why the old-fashioned vinyl pull-ons (or any other vinyl cover) I must graciously *not* recommend. They do not last or launder well, and the pull-ons particularly leave nasty red marks on baby's skin. They are cheap, though—and this is why. Pull-ons have made monumental strides in construction, durability, and quality, and what is currently available has made the old, three-pack, grocery-store type pant *obsolete*. If you do like pull-ons I would recommend wool soakers or a sturdy cotton-urethane, nylon, or poly blend. Each kind has nice bindings which are soft and do not excoriate the skin. Certain snap styles function very much like pull-ons but are easier to take on and off.

Diaper Cover Features

- *breathability:* wool, Gore-Tex/Ultrex, PolarFleece, microfleece
- *durability:* polyester, polyurethane, fleece
- *ease of use:* all-in-ones
- *ease of washing:* polyurethane, polyester, fleece
- *less Velcro problems:* bikini styles, snap, tie-ons, pull-ons
- *waterproofability:* all will have this if handled strictly according to manufacturer's directions; wool and treated all-cotton tend to be more water-*resistant* than water*proof*
- *least expensive:* this depends on sales and volume purchases, but pull-ons and nylon Velcro per piece tend to be least expensive
- *not recommended:* anything with vinyl

Vinyl also emits "outgassing"—vapors from the petrochemical components of the plastic—which can make people sick. (I get headaches from smelling the stuff.) Some people still swear by these, but I believe it's because they're not aware of the recent improvements in diaper cover products today.

Other features to be considered are things like designs or prints on the outer fabric, size of gusset (that little extra piece of fabric on the side of the leg opening that keeps everything inside staying there), strength of Velcro, fit, style, and price.

On Velcro

Some people just don't like the sound Velcro makes. It can definitely shock out a newborn baby! (Try ripping more slowly or do it in short, little pulls.) Another point to consider is that Velcro is strong because it is abrasive, and I have had it rub on my baby's legs or stomach and leave a kind of rub burn there. Some companies sell a Bikini-type with a smaller Velcro patch which helps reduce the likelihood of rubbing, as well as a type of Velcro with a kinder, gentler "rough part."

I find this softer Velcro to be less hearty and durable than the old, stronger kind but if excoriation is a concern look for these. It can also be a matter of how you wrapped the cover on your baby—Velcro rubbing can be avoided if you watch for it. Some covers only use snaps for these reasons, and this is why some parents prefer pull-ons. And the snaps of today are tough plastic, not cold (or hot) metal! They are durable, nice-looking, and a pleasant change from Velcro. Elastic with snaps makes for a firm, snug-fitting diaper and easy-to-use cover.

Some Velcro patches pull off after a short period of time. Some are very strong, some are not. The less-abrasive Velcro seems to be less durable and holds together weakly as a result of the shortened rough part. I give Velcro covers the "yank test" to determine the quality of the Velcro. This variable can really make or break a cover. Can it handle a couple of good yanks after it's fastened to baby? It should stay put and not give way.

Adult and youth diapering

Several fine companies and sources exist for incontinence needs for older children and adults. You can get fitted Velcro or non-Velcro styles and pull-on covers for virtually any size person. In the long run, a rather expensive initial purchase would pay for itself, because over time paper throwaway products are much more costly. Your expense may be covered by Medicaid or other insurance, depending on your

Making Diaper Covers Last Longer

- Resew Velcro as needed
- Remove old Velcro and replace (the rough part gets full of debris sometimes, peels off, or loses stickability)
- Use Seam Sealer where needed on bonded waterproof fabrics such as polyurethane, Gore-Tex, Ultrex, and coated nylon (See Appendix B)
- Lanolin rubbed into wool covers restores and improves natural water-proofability
- Hand wash and line dry covers as much as possible; air dry cover between uses if wet but not soiled
- Never use bleach, and use mild detergents without grease-releasers or other harsh agents if your covers are "sensitive"
- Buy a few extra covers per size and get more mileage from each
- Try an old toothbrush or toothpick to comb out debris in Velcro patch

state and policy. You will be much more comfortable in a cloth product than scratchy, mushy, expensive paper and plastic.

These companies assure the customer of discreet, understanding phone and customer service. Items can also be shipped in unmarked packages for your privacy. Please see the complete listings for adult and youth incontinence products following the Resource listings in Appendix A.

Recommendations

Nothing works for everyone. And you may find the diaper system you use at one point will modify as needs, situations, finances, or time constraints change.

I have found, generally, that how much a cover costs is a good indication of how well it is made and how long it will last. You may buy cheap to begin with and end up spending again and again later. The better-made covers should last for a second baby—some even a third! Consider this when comparing prices as well as features.

Many companies offer great sample deals which allow you to buy one of, say, five different kinds of diapers, or covers, or combination, so you can really experiment and find what works for you. I would take advantage of this where possible. Many companies also offer a single sample of whatever at a reduced price. And don't be afraid to tell them what didn't work (or what did) and why—these companies really appreciate your input, do wish to see you succeed at diapering, and do make changes based on what you tell them!

I must urge you, no matter what system you ultimately choose, to *follow washing instructions exactly*. This way you don't end up with a melted wad of nylon, or a shrunken wool cover, or leaky polyester, after a wash or two! Read carefully before you buy, or ask before you buy.

The next chapter deals with all the accessories you may or may not need for diapering. These items have been designed to make your life easier by improving or refining some aspect of the diapering experience. You will be able to find who sells the products you are looking for by looking in the product index which follows the Company and Resource Guide.

CHAPTER 3

The Other Stuff You Need

(And Maybe Don't)

So many items are out there to complement, enhance, or complete your diapering needs! I am particularly impressed with recent trends towards healthy products with herbs and minimal chemicals, as well as fine reusable items and earthy, natural-fiber alternatives. As you review your catalogs, it might get a little overwhelming to think you need everything offered! Experience will teach you as you learn and diaper. But lest you think you will be depriving baby if, say, you don't get a wipe warmer, people have done just fine by leaving the wipes on the radiator, or running a washcloth under the hot tap, or whatever, without one. I present a minimalist perspective from which you can branch out purchase-wise if you choose. (See chapter 9 for a complete "What to Buy" list for baby.)

Pins, clips, Snappis

Everyone associates cloth diapers with pins. Yes, they definitely still do exist! The high-quality metal pins made mowadays have asliding head which protects baby and cannot be easily pulled apart In lieu of pins one can use the newfangled diaper clips—these are little squarish things that lock down on the diaper material. If you are an old-fashioned diaperer, these might be better than pins if the idea of sticking your baby con-

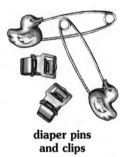

diaper pins and clips

cerns you. These have basically, however gone out of the market at the present time.

An old-timers secret is to sharpen your pins every so often with a sharpening stone and keep them stored in a bar of soap, or a more earthy alternative, beeswax. This keeps them slick and easy to slide into the cotton. Check with an apiary (beekeeper) or candle-maker in your area. Or try a candle!

A third alternative is a state-of-the-art clip device called the Snappi. This is a three-pronged plastic gizmo which actually grabs the diaper material in three places (left hip, right hip, and center) and locks onto it, securing the diaper around the baby. New to America, the Snappi sells by the tens of thousands per month in South Africa (where it originated), Australia, and Brazil, and is also expanding into Canada, the United Kingdom, Scandinavia, and other European countries. It's too big for baby to choke on (though the prongs are sharp), and less easy to lose than a pin or a clip. It can provide a good fit without having to use Velcro diapers (if you are a Velcro hater). The Snappi works best with birdseye-weight, flannel, or lightweight gauze

diapers (it needs something it can sink its "teeth" into), though I have managed well enough with diaper service diapers. It also tends to work better on smaller babies, rather than larger, active toddlers.

Since the Snappi is so new to us Americans (Canadians have had it a while already), I encourage all you diehard pinners and clippers to try one! (It may take a little while to get used to, but once you figure it out, it's easy.)

Snappi diaper fastener

Liners: throwaway and reusable

Ugh! Dunking diapers! Yes, definitely the grossest part of cloth diapering. Well, here at least is one way to keep that trial of the soul to a minimum. Many parents use a disposable liner of polypropylene, wood pulp fiber, or even a folded paper towel. The idea is that most or all of the poop will fall into the liner which can be lifted out at changing time and simply flushed away. (Be sure that if you live in a rural area your septic system can handle such heavy material.) Then you can just throw the wet-but-not-really-dirty diaper in the bucket, without soaking, until wash day.

The thing to keep in mind is that this liner is the thing that will actually be touching baby's skin, and for most people into cloth diapering, what actually touches the skin is very important. They like the softness of cotton. So if you're using a synthetic or paper liner, you may find that you love cloth diapering but are willing to forego the softness part for a little less hassle.

Hydrogen-peroxide-bleached and unbleached paper liners are a good alternative, though the unbleached liners tend to be a little rough (bleaching softens as well as whitens the paper fiber).

Another fantastic diaper liner alternative is the rice paper liner—similar to a wood pup liner but made from rice pulp. These smell beautiful (like something earthy), they are very soft, can be resused if not soiled, and are relatively inexpensive.

flushable, unbleached diaper liners

Two things you could do instead: use the disposable liner for a certain part of the day (if your baby poops pretty regularly each morning or whatever) and then go liner-less the rest of the day. Or use a cloth liner or doubler, laid on top of the diaper, which you would end up dunking instead of a whole diaper.

Single layers of flannel or other soft cotton could be cut into narrow strips, edged, and made into reusable liners.

The diaper bucket and bucket liners

For disposable users, one diaper bucket that would be total anathema to any environmentalist seals each diaper in an individual bag so you never smell the diapers again. You empty a bunch of little plastic balls into the weekly trash.

Your diaper service and several companies offer the large (44 quart) bucket that can hold a week's worth of diapers. Unless you plan to wash yourself at home once a week (which I really do not recommend; I recommend every two to three days), are using a service, or have two in diapers, you don't need this big bucket. Many standard buckets exist which hold a few dozen diapers at a time. Some have a charcoal-activated divider or other mechanism to keep odor down. Try to get one with a locking lid if baby becomes too curious! You can use a plastic kitchen garbage liner inside, and then dump everything in the machine on wash day. You toss the liner and save yourself the trouble of rinsing the bucket. A more ecological, economical alternative are the waterproof, reusable liners offered by some companies—these you throw in with the diapers and replace when clean and dried.

Changing pads and bed pads

If you are looking for a changing pad separate from what might be found with your diaper bag, get one of a hefty, washable nylon, or see chapter 10 on making your own.

The nicest bed pads are wool, but some have a heavy flannel top layer which is nice and soft. As I hate plastic stuff for babies, try keeping away from it for bedding items, too. Let them sleep on nice, wholesome things!

The Diaper Duck and Little Squirt

Maybe you think I am sub-mental or something, but I could never figure out how the Diaper Duck is supposed to work. This weird-shaped plastic gizmo enables you to soak a diaper without getting your hands wet, but I have always gotten my hands wet. It's been selling for over 30 years, so most people must figure it out. Oh, well.

Diaper Duck

The Little Squirt water spray is like a little power washer for your diapers. It attaches to the side of the toilet, and you use it to power-rinse any soil off your diapers before storing them. Look in the product index for the exclusive U.S. distriutor.

Deodorizers

Virtually all deodorizers don't really deodorize, except the DeoDisk. This is the one used exclusively by diaper services, and you've got to get through a whole week with a nice smelling house. These really work and I recommend nothing else. They are non-toxic so don't worry about the baby-eating-the-deodorizer myth. Your diaper service will give you as many as you need or want, and they can be purchased through mail-order as well.

Changing tables

Would babyhood be complete without one? Well, we had one too, for the first baby, but what's out there is poorly made, with cheap (and ugly) vinyl or fake-looking wood. Maybe you could get a carpenter or cabinet maker to design you one with shelves and drawers to suit your size needs or whatever, but many people do fine with a nice low dresser. They are roomy, the right height, and have many other practical uses later. Baby's items stay dust-free and uncluttered-looking in a dresser drawer. Minimalists (as I have become) change baby wherever it is convenient, keeping a good changing pad around. You eventually get used to changing baby even without a changing pad.

Chapter 9 discusses creative ideas for setting up your changing area.

Ditty bags

You really *can* use cloth on the go. I often do, depending on the situation. A waterproof, well-made ditty bag of nylon or polyester is a real lifesaver for putting soiled diapers or other wet stuff in until you get home. I like toggles on the end to keep everything inside. If you forget your ditty bag, plastic grocery bags will do, but they lack a certain aesthetic presence.

On the diaper bag

There are such ugly bags out there! Patterned pastel vinyl things which look and wear like a tacky high chair. They crack, don't hold much, stain and rip easily, and *look* like a diaper bag—not nice for the man in your life to walk around with!

Ah, but you should see the diaper bags I've found! Beautiful, durable, cleanable,

nylon diaper bag

practical. Fabrics range from cordura nylon (my favorite) to cotton duck to parachute nylon to denim. Cordura lasts forever and is made for things like camping gear which take a lot of abuse. These bags have better colors, too—solids, happy jewel tones, darker shades which don't show dirt or wear and look nice for Papa to carry around. Unfortunately what's in the stores is most often the worst quality of what's available!

There are bags which are a variant of the backpack. Some are "designer" or executive, for the mother with a job outside the home, with plenty of room for breast pumps and paraphernalia. Others are super-large and hefty for travel; others have special compartments and places for things you need. Hip bags keep your busy hands free. Oh, I would never go back to those ugly vinyl things ever again!

Furthermore, any good, roomy, durable bag you already have can be a diaper bag, if you add a homemade or purchased changing pad.

Another way to save money and keep things simple.

So before you or a gift-giving friend or relative buys the first thing on the shelf at you-know-where, order a couple of catalogs from the Company and Resource Guide and see the ones I'm talking about! You will be pleasantly surprised!

Cleaning agents

This seems like a very personal area, like what kind of deodorant you use. Use what gets your diapers and diaper covers as clean as you like, as long as it is something the catalog or manufacturer says you can use.

There are standard things in the store (which work very well) and alternative, "green" laundry products, free from things like formaldehyde (a preservative), and perfumes. (Frankly, I *like* my diapers to smell good!)

Many parents are rightly concerned about using any more chemical agents than absolutely necessary for their families, and have found low-impact, environmentally-friendly cleaning agents to replace the old familiar ones. The product index has a nice list of companies which offer these alternatives.

The wipe warmer

This is a little heating pad which wraps around your box of commercial baby wipes to keep them warm. You can fill an empty wipe box with water and reusable wipes and a little mild soap and use it that way. If your changing area is in the bathroom or you can otherwise get a warm cloth before changing, you shouldn't need to be bothered with this item.

wipe warmer

Ointments and creams

Another highly personal area. Things can run from simple, earthy products with few ingredients to concoctions out of advanced Chemistry 101! You can find ingredients like cod liver oil, zinc oxide, beeswax, Vitamin E oil, aloe vera, chamomile, calendula, lanolin, vegetable oils, or other pleasant, familiar-sounding things. Or how about this partial list of substances which may be lurking in your baby products? Dicaprylate/dicaprate, disodium EDTA, BHT, polysorbate 20, 2-Promo-20/nitropane, 3-Diol, methylchloroisoth-iazolinone, cocoampho carboxygylcinate, choleth-24, celeth-24, propylene gycol, pentadecalactone, sodium hydroxymethylglycinate. Yes, a lot of these ingredients are preservatives "to keep products fresh and pure." So it can sit on a store shelf for a year before you buy it?

It's no wonder, after that partial roll call, why so many parents who combine disposables with chemical-laden baby wipes, or oint-ments, have babies with chronic diaper rash. Combine stuff like that with a hot, unbreathable disposable, and you've got trouble!

And again I have to ask you: does your baby really need all of that unpronounceable stuff on his skin, when simpler and more whole-some alternatives are available?

Parents, please read your wipes, baby powder, and baby oint-ments carefully. Try to purchase the ones with the fewest chemical ingredients and the most natural and wholesome ingredients. Check out alternative products through mail-order or health food stores. Or go minimalist. Use reusable baby wipes with a little liquid soap like the pure and simple Dr. Bronner's Baby Castile (available at most health food stores and some mail-order sources. The label on the bottle is kind of weird, with references to esoteric rabbinical theolo-gy, but you can always peel it off). Or mineral-oil-free baby oil. Or "unpetroleum" jelly. Or herbal baby creams. Keep things to a mini-mum on baby's tender, sensitive skin and you both will be happier and healthier.

On baby wipes

I often use paper towels instead of disposable baby wipes for trav-eling, and just wet as I need to. (Always carry water in the car with children!) Or wet some paper towels and put in a Ziploc bag before going out. Or buy disposable wipes with minimal chemical ingredi-ents. Or use reusable baby wipes. You can stick a couple of wet, soapy ones in a Ziploc bag. I basically use thin, cheap Woolworth-type spe-cials for washcloths and baby wipes. I get a dozen for a couple of bucks and the thin terry really does a great job of cleaning. Plush terry doesn't work as well because it is actually too thick to reach all those little folds of skin!

See chapter 10 for some make-your-own baby wipes recipes.

DIAPER CHANGES

Baby powders

Some authorities say talc is out, because babies can breathe it and it's bad for the lungs and may be contaminated with asbestos. Some say cornstarch is out, because it promotes bacterial growth. Others say cornstarch is in, because it absorbs moisture without talc's bad effects.

I would say that if you can avoid putting anything, including powders, on a new baby, so much the better. When they get older you might see how their skin responds to a little powder of your choice. Don't sprinkle talc in baby's face—put into your hand first and then smooth on. In hot weather I did see powders affect my babies—they got little bumps and so on. You would have to see what your own baby tolerates. Do use ones with minimal chemical ingredients— many are just powder and fragrance.

A cheap alternative would be plain old cornstarch from the baking section of the store, used plain or mixed into another container with half talcum baby powder. Cheaper than store brands! Try an old plastic salt shaker with a lid. Alternative, clay or arrowroot-based powders are also available, free of both talc and cornstarch.

The herbal difference

I am so grateful to be discovering the lost art of treating bodily needs through the plants that grow around us. I've used herbal teas for pregnancy, nursing, to help me to go to sleep, and herbs too, to treat bad skin lacerations, oncoming colds and flu, even diaper rash. Join me as we look at a couple of naturally healing herbs. (None of the information here is given as any kind of prescription or medical advice, of course—rather for your intelligent discretion!)

calendula
calendula officinalis

The leaves and flowers of the calendula plant are used as a salve for wounds and other skin conditions.

Calendula is actually a kind of marigold with known skin-healing properties. Many of your herbal baby cream and ointment preparations will contain calendula, as well as plant and nut oils such as olive, jojoba, safflower, sweet almond, and vitamin E (which is really an oil).

Plantain is another skin-healing herb which, believe it or not, grows in your yard! Try looking close to the ground for its oval leaves with veins running through. People have used a crushed and wetted leaf poultice on baby's sore area and

plantain
plantain major

This grows in your yard! People have crushed fresh leaves (or made a poultice) and used it on scratches, wounds, cuts, sores, insect bites, and even hemmorroids.

then diapered as usual. Reports of toxins being drawn from the body and even deeply imbedded splinters coming out have been reported with the use of plantain.

Aloe Vera is that popular tropical houseplant with a thick juice inside the fat stalks, which are its leaves. It is tremendously effective for sunburn and skin irritations of any sort.

Vitamin E comes in little capsules which you can break open and spread on sore skin. It is a nice alternative to regular baby oil (which is mostly mineral oil, a petroleum by-product which many consider to be unhealthy for human skin).

aloe
aloe vera

Break off a stalk and rub the juice on minor cuts or burns, scratches, or other minor skin irritations.

About training pants

So many of them are chintzy, poorly made, unattractive, and not even waterproof, you have to wonder why anyone buys them! Don't bother with those kinds at all. Get one with a real waterproof layer (nylon or polyester) or else your training endeavors will be in vain!

But I never used training pants, and my girls were out of diapers by two and a half. I know this mostly has to do with their wearing cloth for most of their lives, but I wonder if training pants are not just another thing you have to train them out of. For the babies in disposables since birth, perhaps the training pant is the first experience of feeling true wetness, and training really only starts from that point. I just told my girls that after diapers comes *The Potty*. *The Potty* was very special and became a goal and an achievement. There were a few accidents, but everybody has accidents. I am no socio-psycho-physio anybody, just a mother who's been through it.

Swim diapers

Definitely nicer than the overloaded, two-ton disposable when fully saturated with water! Designed to look nice, work like a diaper and no pins needed for water play.

Pottys

Another highly individual matter. And individuality changes not only from family to family, but from child to child. And some children lose interest in one kind of potty mid-stream and then you need to try another. Try to get your child to the regular toilet as soon as possible. This will make life easier for you and ultimately for them as well. Some pottys attach to the regular toilet and then you use a step stool. It folds up when an adult needs to use it. Eventually they learn to straddle the big toilet.

An attachable toilet seat is preferable for those with small bathrooms as well.

The following chapters discuss the costs of diapering, plus environmental, health, and safety issues. Ready to get "fully informed?"

CHAPTER 4

The Costs of Diapering

How much does it cost to diaper? Isn't it cheaper just to use disposables, than having to buy a whole bunch of diapers and covers, and then wash them all of the time? And what about a diaper service? If I have more than one child in diapers, it runs into a lot of money, right?

Trying to put together some kind of basic price reference for you has just about made my head spin. What variables do we use? How to compare the apples of disposables to the oranges of cloth?

These are some of the more exasperating elements to contend with: *How long is the diapering period?* (It's obviously longer for some children than others.) *How many times is baby changed?* (This depends on whether you use cloth, which is usually changed more often, or disposables, which parents keep on longer because they feel "drier" when wet. Or perhaps the ideal number of times a diaper is changed versus the real number.) *What kind of products are we talking about?* (The cheap-pee disposables, the "alternative" expensive ones, the mainline expensive ones, bulk purchases, or what? And what about whether you use simple nylon pull-on covers or the cadillac wool Velcro covers, or $100.00 a dozen fitted diapers with fancy styling or plain old prefolds?) And then, *what kind of energy do you use to wash and dry?* And what if your diapers take a long time to dry? And *what about the garbage disposal fees* for hauling away that can of disposables every week?

So this is what I did. I have given some basic parameters, and worked within them. The results are possibilities, rather than absolutes. Everybody who does this pricing thing comes up with results which are a little bit different. Still, nobody has argued the one

SUMMARY OF DIAPERING COSTS

Method	Cost (70 diapers per week)
Home Diapering	5¢ to 14¢ per change $3.50 to $9.60 per week $500.00 to about $1,250.00 for diapering period
Diaper Service	19¢ per change $12.00 to 15.00 per week about $1,730.00 for diapering period (add cost of covers)
Disposables	24¢ per change $16.80 per week about $2,180.00 for diapering period (add cost of garbage disposal)

point about the costs of diapering which holds true no matter how you price it: cloth is cheaper than disposables, sometimes a lot cheaper. Here's what I figured out.

Generalizations

Home diapering can cost as little as $450 or less from birth to training, *or as high as $1,200*, and anywhere in between. Many products are made well enough to be used for a second baby.

Diaper service can cost about $1700, depending on local rates, age of baby, age until toilet training, and types of covers you buy. (Covers will add another few hundred dollars to your total cost for diaper service, depending on the type and quantity of covers you buy.)

Disposables can cost about $2,000, depending on how often you change, the type of disposables you buy, and the age at which baby trains. (Garbage disposal costs over the diapering period will also add a couple of hundred dollars to the total cost.)

Babies are changed more often in the newborn months (ten to twelve times a day or more) and eight times a day or less as they get older. Generally, a baby trains at about two and a half, going through about

The Costs of Diapering

9,000 diaper changes (an average of 70 diapers a week, every two to three hours), more in the newborn months, and less in toddler years.

A disposable-diapered baby gets changed somewhat less often, owing to the gels which make the diaper feel dry when it is wet. Babies should, for their health, be changed every two to three hours, or every three to four hours at most for toddlers. My stats are based on what should be, not what people get away with.

It also seems some disposable-diapered babies are training later, due to the use of ultra diapers. This would increase the length of the diapering period, and thus the cost, for these babies.

Keep in mind that many parents use a combination of disposables and cloth diapers.

I based all costs on a diapering period of two and a half years (130 weeks) and an average of 70 diaper changes a week (every two to three hours), or about 9,000 changes in total.

Diapering at home

The cost of home diapering involves 4 main variables: diapers, diaper covers, detergent, and energy (washing and drying). Diapering has come a long way from the chintzy, fold-and-pin/vinyl pant thing of past generations. So today, you pay more for better quality products. In the long run, you save money, because these costs are always far less than disposables, and the better made products can be used for more than one baby. And you won't wear out midstream and need to buy cheaply again.

Diapers

You can't spend less than $20 to $25/dozen and get decent diapers. The less expensive ones you have seen at the local grocery or superstore are inferior products which I do not recommend. (See chapter 3 for a complete discussion of various types of diapers.)

The $20 to $25/dozen diapers are usually diaper service quality prefolds or perhaps some green cotton varieties. Then there's another category in the $30 to $40/dozen range, and another in the $50 to $60/dozen range and the highest in the $100/dozen range. These higher-priced diapers tend to be various types of fitted, contour, or some flannel/terrycloth combinations. However, unless you really fall in love with a more expensive type diaper, you will in no way be depriving your baby with the $20 to $25/dozen kind!

35

DIAPER CHANGES

I have used a figure of five dozen diapers to purchase, because that's the most anybody would really need for one baby. Many parents do fine on three dozen, or less. It all depends on how often you plan to wash.

So, for *five dozen diapers,* you can spend:

- *$100 to $125/dozen for really good diapers*
- *$150 to $175/dozen in the higher cost range*
- *$550/dozen for the highest priced diapers*

Again, unless there is a particular feature you really like in a very high-priced diaper, the "really good diapers" are fine—actually excellent, and far better than *anything* you will find in the regular store.

Diaper covers

I use a figure of twenty-five covers total, five for each size. Some brands and styles use only two or three sizes, but this is what you're most likely to see.

So, for *twenty-five diaper covers,* you can spend:

- *$4/piece, $100 total* (low-end, good quality)
- *$6 to $11/piece, $150 to $175 total* (better to high quality)
- *$17 to $18/piece, about $450 total* (premium or specialty covers)

About all-in-ones

This modern invention combines the diaper and the cover into one unit—and combines diaper and covers costs as well. *For $10 to $12/piece, you can furnish yourself with six dozen all-in-ones (two dozen per size) for $700 to $850* or so. These you will have to launder every couple of days or so and this price depends very much on how often you plan to wash.

Many parents use all-in-ones as a supplemental, rather than primary diapering system, to save money.

Detergents

I averaged two popular cleaning combinations: Tide/Borax and Dreft/Borax at two loads per week for 130 weeks. If you like special cleaning agents or live in a more expensive area than I do you'll probably be paying more. Please also note that some diaper covers cannot tolerate the products I used for pricing examples.

Detergents can cost 34¢ a load, or under $100 for two and a half years.

Energy

Some of you use gas, oil, coal, or perhaps solar energy to heat your hot water, so take this into consideration when comparing with the following electricity rates.

The national average for a wash (hot wash/cold rinse) is 19¢, and to dry (one hour on hot) is 40¢, according to the National Electric Power Research Institute's 1995 figures. *Energy use can cost about 60¢ per load, $1.20 a week for two loads, and about $150* for 130 weeks.

Whenever you line dry, you cut your energy costs by 60 percent.

If you will be using thick, heavy diapers, expect longer drying times.

If you use a laundromat, figure your costs based on whatever size machine your load will need, plus however many minutes it takes to dry. All laundromats are different.

Detergents plus energy

I find that *cleaning agents plus energy can cost about $250 total* for the entire 130 week, two-and-a-half-year diapering period. This does not include the cost of paying for water, if you have to, depreciation on the washer and dryer, etc.

In total

For *five dozen diapers, twenty-five diaper covers, and two loads a week* to wash and machine dry for two and a half years, it can cost in the range of:

- $450 *(for a low-cost system); about $3.50 a week; about 5¢ per change*
- $600 *(for a mid-end system); about $4.50 a week; 6¢ to 7¢ per change*
- $1,250 *(for a high-end system) about $8.00 a week; 13¢ to 14¢ per change*

Your *home diapering system,* based on 9,100 diaper changes over two and a half years, can cost from about *5¢ to about 14¢* a

Home Diapering: At a Glance

	Low	Medium	High
Diapers	$100	$300	$550
Covers	$100	$160	$450
Detergents	$100	$100	$100
Energy	$150	$150	$150
TOTAL	$450	$560	$1250

- Costs based on a two-and-a-half-year (130 week) diapering period
- Low-cost system might be nylon pull-ons and diaper service prefolds
- Mid-end system might be nylon, polyester, or polyurethane covers and contour diapers
- High-end system might be wool Velcro covers and fitted snap or Velcro diapers
- Many parents use diapers from one price range and covers from another (low-end diapers plus high-end covers, for example)
- Prices based on 5 dozen diapers and 25 diaper covers

change, depending how often you wash, cleaning agents used, and the types and quantity of products you buy.

Most parents probably use the low to mid-range quality of diapers and covers, or might use premium covers with $20/dozen diapers. I don't expect too many parents to couple premium diapers with premium covers, but I gave it to show a possible high-end diapering choice.

These estimates are therefore very general and are to be used as a perspective from which to make your own diapering choices.

Your diaper service

The average number of diapers ordered is 70 per week, more when they are newborns, and less as they get older. The average price

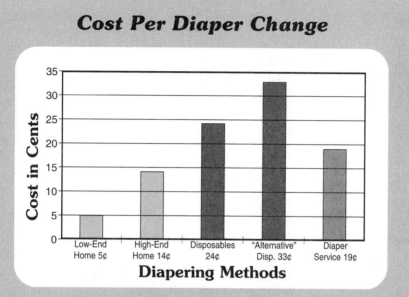

Cost Per Diaper Change

Diapering Methods

- Home Diapering includes cost of detergent, wash and dry, 25 diaper covers, and 5 dozen diapers at two loads a week and based on 70 average changes per week for 170 weeks
- Diaper Service is averaged at $13.50 per week average for 70 diapers and includes cost of home delivery (Add 3¢ average per change for diaper covers)
- Disposables vary in cost by area and style. Price given is based on national average price for Pampers, March 1996 (Add 2¢ average per change for disposal costs)
- Alternative disposables includes cost of home delivery (Add 2¢ average per change for disposal costs)
- All figures are potential rather than absolute

for weekly service runs between $12 and $15 nationally. I average at $13.50 per week.

The costs of using a *diaper service averages out to about $1755* for two and a half years, *and 19¢ per diaper change*. This does not include the cost of diaper covers, which adds another $275 average to the grand total, (3¢ per change), depending on what you'll use.

DIAPER CHANGES

If diaper services are cheaper in your area, or you use less diapers per week, it will be a better deal for you. The price includes pick up of soiled diapers and delivery every week to your doorstep.

Disposables

There are two basic disposable diaper categories. One is the highly advertised, commercial brands which are in every baby magazine and on TV, which have the greater market share overall. Then there are a plethora of generic, store or off-brands. I have found that all disposables, with a few exceptions, basically work the same. A couple of marginal ones leaked or ripped easily, but I believe price has little to do with performance overall.

It is interesting, though, that the disposables currently being touted as "premium" or "supreme" are designed to look and feel like cloth diapers—and even sport Velcro-like tabs! Somebody out there is trying to make you feel more comfortable using disposables—by making them actually cloth diaperish . . . right?

The average price

Based on the national average price of the best-selling disposable diaper in the U.S., *disposables cost about 24¢ per average diaper change, or $2,184 for 9,100 diaper changes* over two and a half years. This assumes a 70/week diaper change (more in newborn months, less as baby grows). This still comes out to about one change every two to three hours—a good, healthy practice. Disposable diaper diary studies which show considerably less than this simply reflect poor diapering practices (and probably an attempt to save money at the expense of baby's health).

Garbage disposal costs add another 2¢ to each diaper change, or about $200 additional to the cost of disposables.

You may find the costs varying somewhat from this, as rural Pennsylvanians (such as I now am) pay only 20¢ per average change, while suburban Californians pay 34¢ per change! This will also depend on the brand, as prices can vary anywhere from 5¢ to 11¢ or more from brand to brand.

An "alternative" disposable

A higher-priced disposable, advertised as "alternative," offers a club price of 33¢ an average diaper change. This is 14¢ more per

Diapering Really Cheaply

- Any of these can be made into diapers: old hand towels (use just as they are); terry towels cut up; flannel sheets or old clothing cut up (see chapter 10 for diaper patterns).
- Purchase diapers from the diaper service in your area—the ones they call "rags." These usually have plenty of wear left but are not "perfect" for customer use (may have some rips or stains).
- A garbage bag can be used in a pinch for a diaper cover—just cut to hourglass shape and tie the ends together at sides around baby.
- Ask around. Most moms beyond "diaper years" will be glad to give you their old diapers or covers.
- Frequent garage and yard sales or put an ad in your local paper.
- Go online—the Internet is developing quite a grass-roots used diaper network.
- See chapter 10 and Appendix B for more make-your-own ideas, patterns, and sources.

change than the average diaper service, almost three times the cost of the most expensive home diapering system available, more than six times the cost of a decent low-end home diapering system. That's *$2,300 to $3,000 for a recommended 7,000 to 9,000 changes* (eight to ten per day) over two and a half years.

So think about this

Cloth diapering at home will cost you one quarter to one half the cost of disposables or less, primarily depending on the types and quantity of covers you buy. Diaper services cost somewhat less than disposables overall. The "alternative" disposable will cost you over 10¢ more per diaper change than either a diaper service or a regular disposable, and about three to six times the price of any home diapering system.

CHAPTER 5

The Environmental Realities of Diapering

What's all the fuss about what diaper to use? Aren't disposables and cloth a tie when it comes to the environment? Cloth diapers are just for radicals and old fogies, but not for the twenty-first century, right?

A fully informed choice

The information in this chapter is provided to enable you to make a "fully informed choice" between cloth and disposables. I want you to sift through ad campaigns and rhetoric, and see for yourself whether or not disposables and cloth are truly an environmental "tie score," as some have suggested. I think you will be surprised that there is any debate about diapers and the environment at all, when all the facts are looked at together!

DISPOSABLES

Have you ever considered what disposables are made of? Did you ever wonder how disposables get so perfectly white? Have you ever thought about what happens to a disposable diaper after it leaves baby's bottom and goes into the garbage?

How many disposables?

Eighteen billion disposables are generated each year in the United States, which amounts to over a ton of garbage for every baby in his diapering period. In total this huge amount of garbage could be laid end to end and go to the moon and back (240,000 miles) several

The Three Diapering Methods Compared

Home Diapering	Diaper Service	Disposables
• by far the lowest price	• the ultimate in convenience	• good for traveling or other special circumstances
• greatest control over types of products used on baby	• the cleanest, whitest, most sterile diapers available	• solid waste (landfill) and other environmental issues far from resolved
• does not contribute to the solid waste problem	• lower or competitive in price with most disposables	• questionable and unhealthy chemicals used in most disposables
• no unhealthy chemicals to worry about	• may be the most energy-efficient option and use the least amount of water	• you pay for hidden disposal costs as well the general high price for disposable use
• most work involved (time and personal energy)	• does not contribute to the solid waste problem	
• aesthetically the most appealing option	• the other aesthetically appealing option	• aesthetically the least appealing option

times! It has been said that the amount of disposables we Americans generate in just one year could fill twenty-five football fields thirty stories high!

Lots of stats

Imagine one garbage barge filled just with disposables, generated every six hours, for 322 days! 410 tons an hour! 9,680 tons a day! It's not hard to believe, then, that disposables make up the third largest single consumer item in the waste stream, after newspapers and beverage containers. They also amount to 2 to 3 percent of the total amount of solid waste, and 30 percent of the non-biodegradable waste. (Disposable diapers are non-biodegradable because landfills lack the light and air needed to allow anything within them to truly degrade.)

Does it really matter at all?

Some feel diapers needn't be singled out as a major environmental threat when it is only a small part of a whole throwaway lifestyle. Others feel that every area with environmental impact needs to be examined, especially with an item as ubiquitous as the disposable diaper, and efforts made to reduce waste wherever possible.

Landfill space is currently at a premium—remember the famous New York barge without a country floating around in the ocean, with no place to dump the tons of disposables it contained?

Composting and recycling

Disposable manufacturers have experimented with recycling and composting but these remain largely theoretical because they are expensive to implement, not universally available, and the public simply isn't ready for these measures yet. And although disposables have gotten thinner over the years and would conceivably take up less room than in a landfill than they used to, they continue to be used in greater numbers, particularly overseas.

Landfills and leachate

It has been reported that pathogens like viruses have been found in the landfill sites, but others would say they don't survive long enough to cause any really danger to anyone. Others have contended that disease may be spread by birds, rats, or flies which frequent landfills—or that pollutants seep out (the stuff is called *leachate*), potentially contaminating groundwaters nearby.

Landfills are better constructed now, however, than they used to be, leak less than they used to, and are capped to cover and contain their garbage.

But many people just don't like the idea of human waste, which is better dealt with through the sewage system or septic or whatever, being left to fester in landfills. Should feces really be there at all?

Sometimes I think of wads of mummified excrement sitting buried for generations. Or seagulls picking at rotting, stinking filth as a barge meanders its way to whatever dump it may load its mess at. Something to think about!

> ## CLOTH FACTS
> - Cloth is reusable.
> - Cloth does not add large burden of solid waste.
> - Cloth is cheaper.

How we get the fluffy stuff

Disposables are made mostly of soft, fluffy wood pulp, which comes from chemically treated wood fiber. Environmentalists say that this is the first strike against disposables—using our forests—whether farmed or not—to create a single use, rather than reusable, diapering product.

Additionally, the pulp undergoes a whitening and softening process which, in the traditional method, exposes the pulp to what are known as "chlorine-based bleaching agents," such as chlorine gas and chlorine dioxide. These paper-making methods produce a multitude of toxic, chemical by-products that are released into the environment during manufacturing.

Organochlorines and dioxin

When these agents are used to make the paper for a disposable, substances called organochlorines are produced; these are among the most dangerous, unwanted by-products. Not only are organochlorines found in large quantities in the manufacturing effluent (waste water released in the environment), but they remain ever-so-minutely after manufacturing in the paper fluff itself. This remains true even with the recent movements towards processes which significantly reduce the creation of organochlorines, such as chlorine-dioxide bleaching.

One of the well-known and nefarious organochlorines is the dioxin group, which some of you might remember from the Vietnam War and its connection to Agent Orange. Dioxin has been called the most toxic substance ever produced(!), and has been associated with birth defects, miscarriage, cancer, and genetic damage. No one knows exactly how much exposure to dioxin is necessary for any kind of disease processes to develop, since it is toxic in such small amounts. In countries overseas, safe chlorine-free processes, like hydrogen-peroxide bleaching, is being used for many paper products, including disposables. Chlorine bleaching is actually banned from the manufacturing of disposables in some countries! Such practices have yet to gain real ground here in the United States, although pressure is on the paper industry to reduce and eventually eliminate the use of chlorine in all paper manufacturing.

CLOTH: HOME LAUNDERED AND DIAPER SERVICE

Cloth diapers are a refreshing lesson in positivity after all the concerns associated with plastic and paper diapers!

Reduce, reuse, recycle

Both sides of the debate agree that it takes far less land and raw materials to make and dispose of that piece of cotton cloth than it does an equivalent plastic-and-paper diaper. Just think of a couple of dozen cloth diapers compared to eight thousand or more disposables!

A cloth diaper produces less landfill waste. And there's usually nothing of a cloth diaper left to get recycled, after it's been used for a couple of years on a baby or two and then used a few more years as a rag!

Cotton's not perfect . . . but getting there

Cotton, however, is a highly-pesticide laden crop, and cottons for diapering are usually bleached well and must continue to be bleached, as people squirm away from stained diapers. The environmental impact of chlorine bleaching paper products is far greater, however, than the chlorine bleaching of diapers in a service or at home.

Cloth diapers must also be laundered, and this does make its own impact in terms of detergents, water, and energy consumption. Reputable critics of the studies have concluded that even this environmental toll is far less than that engendered by the use of disposables.

Two new trends have emerged in this decade which show great promise for cloth diapers approaching nearly perfect environmental friendliness: organic cottons and green cottons (sometimes blessedly combined!).

Cotton grown organically leaves off pesticides, herbicides, fungicides, and defoliants in the growing phase; cotton produced "green"

Why You Should Use a Diaper Service

Why should you use a diaper service? Because it makes life so much easier! If you are new to cloth diapering, it will be your very best start— no overwhelming amount of extra laundry and work, and nothing beats the beautiful look and fresh smell of those carefully folded bundles arriving at your doorstep every week! If you are a veteran cloth diaperer, you may find times when having the work done for you is welcome relief within the complexities of a busy lifestyle, whether you work from home, at home, or outside the home.

Convenience

- I feel like a queen every week when the guy takes all my dirty diapers away and leaves these nice plastic bags full of soft, sweet-smelling, lovely whiteness. All I do is tie the bag, put it out the door, write a check, and relax. During the week I merely shake any solid waste I can into the toilet, then throw the diaper in the bucket. Simple! If it's very hot and humid you may want to rinse the diaper first, but the services definitely say you don't need to do this. Then you wash your diaper covers with your next laundry load, or hand wash, depending on the kind of covers you have. (See Chapter 2 for cover types and washing guidelines.) Some diaper services even wash the covers for you.

Postpartum

- I love a diaper service especially right after the birth of the baby. You don't have to juggle an extra load or two a week to your already burgeoning laundry pile. You should do everything to make life easier on yourself, especially in the often-overwhelming postpartum period!

Cost

- The costs are generally less than using disposables over the diapering period, even with the purchase of covers. Some services even rent diaper covers to you (for as little as 25 cents a week a piece) so you don't have to buy a whole bunch of covers all at once.

omits chlorine-based bleaches during manufacturing which make cotton that perfect white so many people love. Furthermore, for the lovers of the perfectly white cotton diaper, fibers can be lightened with the use of hydrogen peroxide, an environmentally friendly alternative.

- You can pay for service by the week or by the month. The service in my area gives the 7th week free if I pay for six weeks up front!

Health

- The Diagard process (the name some services use for their laundering process), with 13 wash and rinse cycles, plus monthly testing of random diaper samples, ensures perfectly germ-free, sanitized diapers. If you have any problems with rashes, your diaper service can even help you by adjusting the pH of your own batch of diapers (for no additional charge). This often helps babies having rashes due to teething or trying new foods.

Environment

- I feel so good and right about using a diaper service. Though home-washing your own diapers is certainly better for the environment than using disposables, it takes less water and energy to wash one diaper-service diaper than one of my own home-washed ones. Plus services re-use the final rinse water as the wash water for the next load. And some services are starting to use environmentally-safe hydrogen-peroxide bleaching instead of the much-maligned chlorine for bleaching.

Aesthetics

- Lovely, soft, sanitized, clean, durable sweet-smelling white diapers, every week, with no work.

The modern answer

- Since it doesn't cost any more to use a diaper service than it does to use disposables, since it is better for the environment, since cloth is better for your baby's health, since services do nearly all the work for you, since the diapers are so clean, sanitized, and pure, WHY NOT USE A DIAPER SERVICE?
- Please consult your local telephone directory for the diaper service or services in your area.

Diaper service: our earth's diapering friend

The diaper washed through a diaper service, amazingly, undergoes thirteen changes of water from start to finish, yet uses less water per diaper than you would at home in one normal laundry load! And though the official studies were not in solemn agreement, respected diaper service research showed that services use less water and energy than disposables or home laundering overall.

BETWEEN THE TWO:
ADVERTISING, STUDIES, LAWSUITS

The course of modern diapering

The use of disposable diapers birthed and skyrocketed in the 1960s but came to a halt in the late 1980s when the media drew attention to the landfill crisis in America. It seemed that people everywhere began to take notice of the environment, with "green" and "environmentally-safe" designations popping up everywhere, and parents using diapers went along with this newfound sense of environmental duty. A Gallup poll from 1990 found that one quarter of the U.S. population was willing to switch to cloth to help the environment!

Why switch?

After the first couple of years in the 1990s, cloth diaper use had tapered off again. Why was this, after diaper services had phones ringing off the hook and business was booming for them, especially in the late 1980s and early 1990s?

No environmental winner?

I remember the ad well. It was 1992, and I was reading one of those baby magazines. "90 days ago (or whatever), this was a disposable diaper." It showed a tree with roots smothered in luscious black compost. Ah, so a disposable goes back to the earth and helps make trees grow, right?

Then there were these nice little brochures coming in the mail, describing a "closer look" at disposables. Doctors and studies were quoted, enthusiastically heralding disposables as superior to cloth for baby's health and not any worse for the environment than cloth. Wow! So I don't have to wash diapers after all, to ease my environmental conscience? And now they've even got disposables that look and act like cloth diapers, so it gets even better, right?

These ad campaigns were very successful, extremely successful, in halting what was becoming a mass exodus from the disposable diaper. I think many parents earnestly want to do what's best for their baby and the environment, too—and simply believe what they are told. And when you've got multimillion dollar advertising budgets and direct marketing capabilities of the highest order, you certainly can get any message out that you want, and get people to believe it!

Hey, wait a minute, Mr. Ad-man!

There has been quite a bit of backlash to the various advertising strategies, coming from scientists, lawmakers, and environmental groups. Unfortunately, little of this counter-offensive seems to have made any difference in the realm of public opinion and public action at this time.

Lifecycle analyses

First of all, four major studies, called "lifecycle analyses" were conducted in the late 1980s and early 1990s to try to determine the environmental impacts of cloth diapering—both laundered and diaper service—and disposables. Three of them held the conclusion that though the environmental impacts of cloth and disposables were different, the effects were equal (so go ahead and use disposables without guilt). The fourth determined a quite different conclusion—that disposables created far more environmental damage than cloth diapers, either those home-washed or processed through a diaper service.

The trouble is, that the three studies used to claim an "environmental tie," and "no environmental winner" between either method were commissioned by the disposable diaper industry, and the one to conclude that cloth is environmentally superior was commissioned by the cloth diapering industry.

Naturally, since these studies were "scientific" and all, each side has used studies favorable to itself in advertising, publicity, and public education materials.

The voices of reason

However, neutral voices had arisen—those with no financial or other interest in either industry—which criticized the disposable diaper monolith for features of its ad campaigns and the quality of the research used as a basis for this advertising. Public interest groups have recognized the "subjectivity" of these studies but say that while the diaper service study was credible, the disposable diaper studies were faulty, heavily biased against cloth, and even factually incorrect.

One particularly formidable finding was the report financed in the United Kingdom by the Women's Environmental Network—a neutral advocacy group. This 1991 report prepared by the respected Landbank Consultancy group compared both the Lentz and Little (Proctor & Gamble funded) studies and even used their own statistics, but found that, far from both diapering methods being equal, disposables actually use *"Twenty times more raw material, three times more energy, two times more water and generate sixty times more solid waste"* than do cloth diapers.

Well, so what?

What happened was that after lawsuits in many states, as well as action in other countries, the disposable-into-compost ad was prohibited from being used again—but not until millions of parents read it—and believed it!

Composting is available only to 1 percent of the U.S. population so it was deemed misleading to advertise the compostability of diapers when it is not available widely. And nobody can advertise disposables

Think about it—8,000 or more disposables (and over a ton of garbage), or a few dozen diapers and some covers!

as "biodegradable" anymore, no matter how much cornstarch you put in the backing, due to lawsuits against advertisers by environmental groups. The terms used to describe the ad campaign included such lovely epithets as "misleading," "deceptive," "green-washing," and "false advertising."

Furthermore, lifecycle analyses have been criticized as an insufficient medium to truly find out the environmental impact of cloth and disposables. But I have to wonder if some things are better left to common sense rather than endless scientific inquiry!

In perspective

No diapering method, or any other industrial endeavor, is without environmental impact. But what will the environmental future hold for the earth if we do not reduce, reuse, and recycle, in as many ways as possible, as often as possible?

CHAPTER 6

The Health and Safety of Diapering

As conscientious parents, you will also want to be aware of some of the health and safety concerns that have arisen related to both cloth and disposable diapering methods.

Chemicals in disposable diapers

Discussed previously, there are two chemical substances that many health advocates feel just shouldn't be in a baby's diaper at all: sodium polyacrylate, and dioxin.

Sodium Polyacrylate

Sodium polyacrylate is the substance within the fluff layer of the disposable that turns your baby's urine into gel—or as I see it, that yucky wad of grossness, that nasty mushiness in the bottom of baby's diaper. This Japanese-licensed chemical can absorb one hundred times its weight in liquid, and has been linked to toxic shock syndrome in tampon use. (Applications are certainly different, but it's certainly something to think about.)

In the past, the use of sodium polyacrylate in ultra disposable diapers had been associated with severe diaper rash and bleeding perineal and scrotal tissue, pulling fluid so strongly as to excoriate it. It has shown up on babies skin as little beads and has been excreted in the urine. It is this same substance, however, which the disposable manufacturers claim gives baby *less* rash than cloth does, because it "keeps baby drier." Maybe too dry!

Although their own industry-funded study says sodium polyacrylate is safe, no neutral long-term study of any kind had been conducted to asses the affect of contact of this substance on sensitive and vulnerable genital tissue over time.

Toilet training

Apparently toilet training troubles are being attributed to the presence of sodium polyacrylate in disposables, as babies diapered in them are training later than usual. It seems that babies need to feel "wetness" in order to train (I guess they're supposed to learn to hate that cold, mushy wet feeling). Also notice that the new disposable "pull-up" training pants are designed to "feel wet"!

Organochlorines

The other consideration within the chemical debate is the presence of organochlorines, including lingering trace amounts of dioxins and furans in the chlorine-bleached paper goods after manufacturing.

What health risks might there be to a baby who has this material on his genitals for the first two and a half years of life? Does the diaper's liner prevent exposure to the trace amounts of clorinated toxic chemicals present in the diaper's fluff? Perhaps. No one knows, however, the exact amount of dioxins and furans necessary to be damaging to our health. We do know, however, that babies are already exposed to significant amounts of these toxins in utero and even through breast milk. Any trace amounts of these chemicals absorbed through disposables must be added to these other sources of organochlorines potentially affecting our children.

Disposable diaper manufacturers are switching to bleaching processes that create less dioxins, but other organochlorines, including furans, are still created and released into the environment every day. The leading disposable manufacturer has stated that dioxin has not been detected in the pulp itself at so many "parts per trillion," but this does not address the other organochlorines, including furans, likely to be present in the disposable's fluff. Furthermore, "non-detect" does not mean zero—it may still linger in minute, though potentially harmful, quantities.

Will we, as some suggest, see cases of scrotal cancer or other diseases attributed to the minuscule presence of dioxin and other organochlorines in disposables, as the disposable diaper generations move into maturity? It is for this reason alone that parents should seriously reconsider the use of disposables, until they are universally made without chlorine. And then, use them sparingly!

Diapers in day care

Centers are finding that they can save money using diaper services and that using Velcro covers for staff makes changing easy. I expect that the use of cloth in all institutions, especially hospitals, will continue to grow as the need to save money and reduce solid waste continues.

And if clothes are worn over cloth diapers, a recent study on day care found that there is no significant advantage of either diapering method over the other in the spread of diarrhea germs.

Synthetics in diaper covers and bedding

Although nylon appears to be the least offensive artificial textile, polyvinyl chloride (PVC, your typical vinyl) and other plastics such as polyester and polyurethane emit "outgassing" of petrochemical components and those who are sensitive to chemical odors or have environmental allergies may find thay get headaches from smelling the stuff. *How do you react to the smell of a new shower curtain?*

PVC not only outgasses vinyl chloride, a "priority pollutant" recognized by the EPA as a health hazard, but it also emits the highly toxic dioxin into the environment during manufacturing.

Poly-cotton blends, nylons, and even some all-cotton fabrics are irremoveably treated with formaldehyde—a suspected carcinogen which can irritate lungs or skin.

Because of these health concerns—what baby is breathing, or touching, and how it might affect him now or in the future, many parents choose untreated cottons and wool for both bedding and diaper covers to complement their all-natural cloth diaper regime.

Diaper rash

The territorial claims to rash prevention are very strong on both sides of the diaper debate. Disposables are advertised heavily as being the best possible thing you could do for your baby's bottom, keeping baby "drier"; diaper service diapers are heralded for their superior bacteria-fighting rinses, breathability, and softness.

As the causes of diaper rash are many, it is probably valid that each shares some claim in preventing diaper rash. I have observed that changing a baby frequently is the best diaper rash preventative going, no matter what diaper you use. This is barring anything like allergies, chemical sensitivities, or illness. Studies from both sides exist which say their diapering method is better for baby's bottom, which

The Diaper Debate:

Statistics:
- 18 billion disposables generated in the U.S. as solid waste every year
- 1 ton of solid waste generated for every baby who uses disposables for entire diapering period
- cloth uses few dozen diapers or all-in-ones, and covers for diapers

Landfill:
- less landfill space than in the 1980s
- disposables contribute 2% of solid waste, 30% non-biodegradable waste
- disposables third largest single consumer item in waste stream
- some see as minor and symbolic; others as vital environmental need to reduce waste

Leachate:
- pathogens exist in landfills but may not survive long
- liquids have been known to seep from sites into local groundwaters
- no definitive study to assess affect of leachate, or rats, flies, and birds spreading disease from landfill sites
- modern sites are capped

Degradability:
- disposable diapers do not degrade in landfills
- cloth diapers basically do not end up in landfills

Raw Materials:
- disposables use more trees, land, and produce more solid waste than cloth
- "green" and organic cotton reduce pesticides and other chemicals in environment—a growing trend in the 1990s

Organochlorines:
- byproduct of chlorine bleaching, traces found in paper products and largely in effluent discharged from pulp mills into waterways
- highly toxic and dangerous to humans
- banned from disposables in other countries
- new methods can significantly reduce dioxins from paper products but are not universally employed in disposable industry; not all organochlorines eliminated with these methods
- intense concern over exposure to dioxin to reproductive organs during first years of life, and in any other way to human life
- green cotton and hydrogen-peroxide bleaching are chlorine-free processes which produce no dioxin at all

Sodium Polyacrylate:
- super-absorbent substance in ultra diapers has in past been associated with rashes, bleeding and other problems
- linked to toxic shock syndrome in tampon use
- disposable diaper industry-funded study says it is safe; no independent long term studies conducted on babies to assess effect of contact on genitals over time

Diaper Rash:
- has probably more to do with frequency of changes than diapering mode
- disposable industry-funded studies do not compare disposables with newer breathable diaper covers

At a Glance

- rashes can be caused by sensitivities to chemicals in disposables, detergents used in cloth laundering or other factors
- most disposable industry funded-studies did not show any overwhelming advantage of disposables over cloth related to diaper rash

Toilet Training:
- baby needs to feel wetness in order to complete toilet training process
- ultra disposables may reduce wetness sensation and contribute to toilet training troubles

The 3 R's:
- Reduce
  —cloth reduces solid waste, use of raw materials and land usage
  —disposables have reduced in volume and thickness over the years
- Reuse
  —disposable cannot be reused at all
  —a cloth diaper can be reused 75 to 300 times
- Recycle
  —neither recycling nor composting of disposables is expected to be in widespread use in the future; though technically possible not economically feasable
  —because cloth already reduces and reuses, recycling is an unnecessary issue

Studies:
- findings seem to favor side funding study in question
- criticism from neutral groups as to validity of disposable diaper-funded studies, both in terms of scientific worthiness and use in advertising
- many areas left unstudied and more information needed

Money:
- home laundered cloth diapers cost one quarter to one half that of disposables
- diaper services somewhat less but comparable to disposables, depending on locality

Safety:
- safety of disposables questionable
- babies have choked on plastic tabs of disposables; one death reported since 1994
- diaper pins and clips are small; if used must not be kept near baby's reach
- natural textile diaper covers avoid petrochemical outgassing of synthetic covers and formaldehyde in polyester blends
- modern cloth diapering methods are pin-free and safe

Convenience:
- a continual purchase of throwaway diapers; the needed trips when you run out, and the extra costs overall
- the idea of convenience needs rethinking
- an extra load or two a week is no big deal, especially with the use of all-in-one cloth diapers
- diaper services, if available, provide the ultimate convenience in cloth diapering

Aesthetics:
- some feel it doesn't matter what we put on babies
- others feel it makes a difference to baby, because cotton would be nicer to wear than paper and plastic for anyone

adds to the confusion. However, since 1994 alone nearly 39 percent of all diaper complaints to the U.S. Consumer Product Safety Commission involved rash or other skin ailments directly related to the use of disposable diapers, and not one similar complaint related to cloth diapers.

My best advice is to change your baby every two to three hours no matter what, and more so if you have any rashes at all. This way any diapering method you choose will be less likely to cause diaper rash. (See chapter 7 for more causes and cures for diaper rash.)

Safety

Reports to the U.S. Consumer Product Safety Commission (CPSC) since 1994 alone have included one death from a baby choking on the tabs of a disposable diaper, and several other incidents of choking on tabs which baby pulled off and put in his mouth. One baby drowned in 1995 when a disposable acted as a flotation device and turned the baby upside down in the water.

Nearly one quarter of the complaints involved rashes caused by disposables, some described as "blisters," "chemical burns," and "dermatitis." Other reports include being "cut," "scratched," and even "scraped by metal filings" found in a disposable diaper.

Some of the odder reports involve objects being found in new disposable diapers, including a piece of wire, sewing needles, a "long metal object," a metal box cutter blade, a "needle-shaped object," and "glass or melted plastic." Even weirder were reports of larvae, worms, dirt and dead bugs found in new packs of disposables.

A number of reports involved "chemical odor" being emitted from the disposable diaper, as well as a "brown spot" suspected to be toxic.

Other reports include gel leaking from the disposable and excess fiber from the disposable inner layer found on baby's crib.

In total, there were forty-four assorted complaints registered with CPSC under disposable diapers between 1994 and October 1996 (just under a three-year period). Conversely, there were only three complaints regarding cloth diapers *in the last sixteen years!*

One child whose cause of death was found to be SIDS was found lying face down on a cloth diaper in his parents waterbed. The only other reported cases were of a five-year-old boy pulling out the mesh lining of a diaper cover and putting it in his mouth, and a fishhook found embedded in the cloth padding of one baby's diaper.

Pins and diaper clips are small and must be kept out of baby's reach. One mother told me of a child who swallowed a diaper pin and it opened up inside his stomach! It is wise to keep a close eye on your baby's often tightly clenched fists for these potential hazards as well as things like lint, hair twisted around, what have you.

The Snappi has sharp teeth which could scratch skin or eyes or hurt your feet if stepped on.

In conclusion

Cloth diapers are better for your pocketbook, the environment, and your baby's health. Diaper services may be the most environmentally-friendly diapering method of all and provide near-disposable convenience. Disposables are expensive, take a greater environmental toll, and are questionable for baby's health and safety. I believe *disposables should be used prudently, cloth more often, and diaper services, whenever available and affordable.*

Now we discuss the nuts and bolts of diapering, and show you how to diaper using various kinds of diapers and folding methods.

CHAPTER 7

How to Diaper

On the act of diapering

The events of mothering happen to us all. Whether or not mothering remains a joy rather than a burden has less to do with circumstances than with attitude. The pregnant mother thinks of little white booties, soft layette things, the caress after baby's first bath, perhaps sitting quietly in her rocking chair in her new robe, reading as baby nurses, listening to calming Baroque strings. The new mother looks at the ever-increasing pile of laundry, another poopy diaper, the dishes left over from last night's dinner, and the loss of sleep over the past several months, and sighs at the new demands and responsibilities. A mother of two, three, or more busily prepares her day's schedule in her head, often gets up before everyone's awake to start defrosting something for dinner, throw the load in the dryer she started last night before she went to bed, start yet another load, and climb back into bed to nurse her youngest before the older ones eagerly rise for breakfast. Then there are diaper changes, and nursings, and art projects, and library trips, and books to read from the library trips, and the playground, and the beach, and the scooter, then the trike, then the bike. It is an ascending spiral in which the simplest events of life remain largely the same while an ever-increasing and broader range of duties and experiences are added to it.

It always saddens me when I see parents who don't seem to enjoy their children or being a parent. Everything is a pain in the neck; the livings and doings are largely a burden; they yearn to run away from it all and often do. Left is an innocent child who has an overriding need to be with, to be held by, to be touched by, to belong to, to be guided by, to laugh with, to be consoled by, nurtured by, taught by, and loved by the same parents who yearn to run away, to get away, to drop them off, to put them to bed.

Ah, but that these parents would let go, accept the total and consuming intensity of loving and being loved by their little ones, and begin to relish performing even the smallest acts of devotion and caring! In this light, in a happy abandonment to the calling of parenthood, can the sometimes unpleasant act of diapering become tolerable, even enjoyable.

Using diapering time

I take the diapering time as time for kisses and hugs and cuddles. With a toddler, time goes by in larger hunks between those loving times, so I grab the chance and give them plenty before getting down to business. I use the time to teach anatomy—"Where's that cute belly button?"—and about bowel functions. They learn it, believe me. When it really reeks we make a big fuss and laugh about it together. They love to see your face get all contorted over something they did. I take note of how the diaper area looks and how the waste looks— any redness, any loose stool? We talk about clothes and diapers and washcloths and getting clean. It's a great "schnoodling" time for very cute bellies and to squeeze soft little butts! Diapering is a great coming together time if you use it that way.

Babies are only that vulnerable for so long—just laying there sprawled out, looking up at you in complete trust. Soon they walk, then run, then get involved with projects, and keep going. You begin to miss simpler times. Do you remember the longing and anticipation of approaching motherhood? Perhaps you are now waiting to hold the baby inside you for the first time. Your longing for motherhood is fulfilled in experiences which are both mundane and sublime.

A joy—all of it

I encourage you to receive motherhood as a joy—all of it—not as a burden or drudgery. Reject the nonsense about two children or twins being "double trouble"—phooey on that! I always said back, "No, quite the contrary—a double *blessing*!" Stop talking about all the things you have to do, how much money you have to spend, how rough life is, and start expressing positive, healthy statements about motherhood—how much you actually enjoy your baby, that you really don't mind what's involved in being a mother, that rather than a hassle, motherhood is a very noble, and satisfying vocation and call-ing. See what I mean? There is so much negativity out there about children it makes me sick!

So use cloth diapers, and say, it's not that much work—besides, I save so much money and help the environment, too. Breast-feed your baby, and keep on going even if people throw the standard deluge of nonsense at you. Laugh or sing with your children in public, and watch people really stare! They can't figure out if you're high or what!

The funny thing about much of the deep things of life is that they are so liquid. Lovemaking involves various liquids. Menstruation and its accompanying fertility involve liquids. breastfeeding is liquid. Childbirth is liquid. Tears are liquid. Wet, moist, and slimy are the fun-damentals of existence!

So have courage and fortitude when you change diapers. Draw confidence from your ability to accomplish so much in a day. Cultivate thankfulness for both the great and small things. And then changing a really stinky, messy diaper—even soaking it!—becomes simply another mature part of a mature parent's day.

Diaper changing for new parents

Even though there are modern and old-fashioned ways to diaper, the basic gist for diaper changing is about the same no matter what you do. Please refer to the diagrams which show you the different folding methods. And keep in mind that everybody folds a little differ-ently.

How often should I change my baby's diaper?

I recommend every two to three hours, and more often if baby is red or has a rash. Most diapers get fully saturated in a couple of hours, and covers start to get moist around the edges. You will have to see how much moisture your diapers and covers can tolerate, and make adjustments accordingly.

You may be able to go longer at night (even eight to ten hours) with an extremely absorbent diaper or two, use of a doubler, and hearty diaper cover. You will have to see how your baby's skin toler-ates having a diaper on this long.

Toddlers can go three to four hours at most between changes, but any longer than this is just not healthy for baby's skin, especially if you are using disposables.

DIAPER CHANGES

Diaper Cover Fold, Velcro or Snap

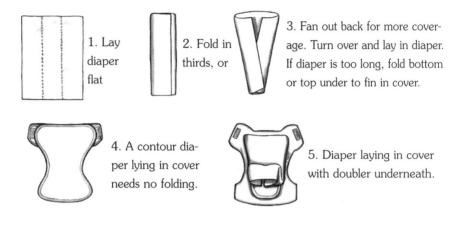

1. Lay diaper flat

2. Fold in thirds, or

3. Fan out back for more coverage. Turn over and lay in diaper. If diaper is too long, fold bottom or top under to fin in cover.

4. A contour diaper lying in cover needs no folding.

5. Diaper laying in cover with doubler underneath.

First

In getting a wet or soiled diaper off, no matter what kind of diapers and covers you use, you want to get the wetness or stool on as little else as possible. With pull-ons you have to *slide* the cover down the legs and off—which can lead to the mess spreading around. This, beyond the extra time a pull-on takes, is probably why most people today use some kind of Velcro or snap diaper and cover combination rather than pins or clips and pull-on covers.

After you've got the thing off, put it on the corner of the changing table, or where baby can't get it. Grabbing the legs "chicken style" keeps the soiled butt from getting on anything and keeps mess on the changing surface to a minimum. With the other hand, get to wiping off as much soil as you can with the first wipe. Then wash out or change sides of cloth and go for the cracks. Don't leave a trace of stool anywhere— check labia well, and under the head of the penis if uncircumcised. Midwives experienced in uncircumcised boys say that the foreskin should be left alone and not retracted to be cleaned. Wipe front to back for both boys and girls.

"chicken legs" changing technique

Diapering for Newborn, Using Regular Prefold

 1. Lay diaper horizontally rather than vertically.

 2. Fold in thirds.

 3. Fold back (for girls) or front (for boys) under to fit, if necessary. Lay in diaper.

Then

Use wipes, plain water (works well for new, breast-fed poop, which actually smells okay), natural baby oils, or a little mild soap like Dr. Bronner's Baby Castile. If you don't use a wipe warmer or other warming method, do try to wet your wipe in warm water first. Reusable wipes go in the bucket with the diapers. If you are using disposables, the most sanitary thing to do is shake any stool into the toilet before disposing the soiled diaper in your garbage pail. (This is, in fact, the method recommended by the manufacturers.)

Stool must also be dumped in the toilet if you are using a diaper service.

Also

The skin should be as dry as possible before putting on a fresh diaper. The time while the skin is air drying is a good time to examine the area for any redness, irritation, soreness, bumps, rashes, what have you. Gently pat dry with the edge of your diaper if you need to. Apply any ointments or natural powders if desired.

Fold, pin, clip, Snappi, wrap, snap, or pull-on according to the kind of diaper and cover combination you will be using.

DIAPER CHANGES

Standard (triple) Fold, for Pins or Clips

 1. Fold left and
right sides in at
a bit of an angle

 2. Fold up bottom portion if
needed to fit baby.

 3. Bring front
panel up
around baby.

4. Pull edges of front panel snugly over sides to overlap and provide a secure fit. Pin or clip through all layers. Keep hand behind
diaper to prevent pin from sticking baby.

Back of diaper may be pulled and overlapped over front panel
instead. (Would work for some pinnable contour styles.)

Diapering at night

It's a good idea to change baby before a night nursing, or any
nursing, if needed, so baby can go to sleep afterward dry and full and
happy. The chill of a wet diaper at night can wake baby. Sometimes
I lay a diaper in a cover and keep it next to our bed so I can change
baby at night while partially incoherent. I take it to the bucket in the
morning.

For younger ones, lay them on top of a waterproof sheet, covered
with something warm, like a receiving blanket, or better yet, a wool
pad of some kind. If the sheet does get wet at night just change in the
morning.

For very heavy wetters, double diaper or use a diaper doubler, and
then put a pull-on cover over whatever other cover you are using, for
extra protection. You may be able to go the whole night this way.

How to Diaper

Old-fashioned Folding Methods

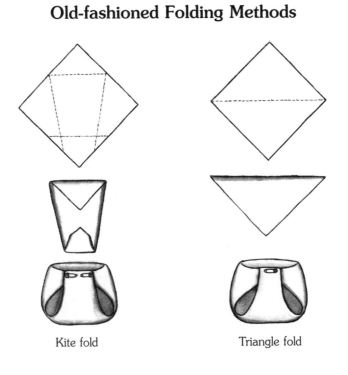

Kite fold   Triangle fold

These are best used with the old style, flat gauze or flannel diapers, square shaped. The triangle fold only requires one pin!

Why does my cover leak?

A frustrating occurence, especially in places where you'd least like it to happen (restaurants, church, in the grocery store, just before a photo shoot . . .)

1. The cover is too big.
2. Your baby's legs are skinny and the opening is too large for his legs. Try another cover style (choices might include pull-ons or bikini styles).
3. The diaper was not fully tucked within the cover.
4. You left the diaper on too long.
5. The cover is getting old, or in washing some of the waterproofing came off or wore off.
5. You did not follow the washing instructions from the manufacturer exactly.

DIAPER RASH

This is a common concern of parents because it does happen so often. What are some of the common causes of diaper rash?

- leaving diaper on too long
- skin not clean enough before fresh diaper is put on
- reaction to detergent, additive, or soaps used to clean diapers or baby
- diaper itself not fully clean or double rinsed
- heat and humidity (especially hot summer days)
- allergies or illness
- sitting in stroller or car seat too long
- using ultra disposable diapers
- a diaper cover that is not breathable enough for your baby
- fungi or yeasts which baby caught from outside source
- teething

I have found that an older child does not poop at night. A completely dry and unsoiled diaper in the morning is a good sign that a toddler is ready for toilet training.

Diapering toddlers

For really big messes, I just stand them in the tub and rinse everything off. Sometimes you can change a busy little guy or girl standing up. Pull-ons are good for a child who has found how to pull their Velcro covers off.

What to buy

Each company you deal with will have its specific version of what you should buy of the products they sell. Some people, for example, might buy the smaller, newborn size diapers for those first few weeks, or if their baby is especially small, and then use them as doublers later when baby outgrows

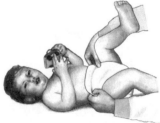

The best method for handling a squirmy baby at changing time is to give him something interesting to hold.

CURES FOR DIAPER RASH

This varies from baby to baby, but here are some basic steps you could take. Please see a health professional if it looks really bad, with bleeding or anything really red, or something which just isn't going away no matter what you do. Use your common sense and motherly intuition.

1. Allow baby to "air out" for as long as possible. Keep him in crib or bed for a while, or let him sleep with no diaper on, just diapers and bed pad underneath him and blanket over him for the night (weather permitting).

2. Lay baby on side or stomach to reduce pressure on buttocks.

3. Get outside in the sunshine and let his diaper area soak up a little sun (weather permitting).

4. Stop all lotions, creams, baby wipes, soaps, powders, detergents, or additives which you think could be making baby sore. Since so many things of this nature can cause a rash, it is all the more reason to keep what you put on baby in the way of chemicals to a minimum. It makes diagnosing a whole lot easier if you have less an array of variables to begin with!

5. Do use some soothing ointment. I have always loved good old Desitin. It usually clears up any minor rash by next morning. For those of you who may not like the cod liver oil in Desitin (though I believe that's precisely what's healing the skin) you might try a calendula cream or other gentle, herbal preparation.

6. Change a baby much more often during the course of a rash.

7. A white vinegar rinse (¼ to ½ cup) in the rinse load, plus a little cider vinegar (¼ cup) in the tub is supposed to help.

8. Change to wool or Gore-Tex/Ultrex covers, which are the most breathable, or go without any covers for a while. Fitted Velcro diapers without covers on would work well in this situation. Baby will need to be monitored.

9. Keep happy and positive, and please see a health professional if all else fails!

them. Others would just use a regular-size diaper folded for a newborn (see diagram). These small differences will affect how much you need to buy of everything overall. In an effort to keep things really simple, I offer a minimalist list of diapering needs, common to everyone. You may find you need less diapers if you do laundry more often, or more diapers if you do laundry less often. Some people need more covers than others, or want to buy more optional items than others.

At least by looking over this chart you can see, very basically, what's involved!

A Simple "What to Buy" List

- 3 to 5 dozen diapers, or 5 dozen all-in-ones, or the use of a diaper service, or a continual purchase of disposables (no covers needed)
- 5 diaper covers per size
- 2 to 3 dozen reusable washcloths, or a continual purchase of throw-away wipes
- a decent diaper bag (see chapter 3)
- 1 to 3 (or more) waterproof ditty bags
- diaper rash cream, ointment, lotion, powder of your choice

Optional:

wipe warmer

changing table

flushable or reusable diaper liners

Diaper Duck or Little Squirt

two bucket liners (one to wash, one to use)

diaper doublers (for night use, heavy wetters, long trips, older babies)

pins, clips, or Snappis as needed

Now let's look at the maintenance aspect of diapering—dealing with dirty diapers and getting them clean.

CHAPTER 8

Laundry Time: Rinsing, Washing, Storing

In the care of cloth diapers the most important factor to consider is the growth of bacteria in the urine and feces and an endeavor to retard this growth until enough of them can be washed at one time to make it worthwhile. This means getting enough of the bladder and bowel material off the diaper as soon as possible, and then storing them somewhere where the likelihood of further bacterial growth is diminished until washing. Ideally all potential pathogens are thus eliminated and diapers are fresh and clean and ready for another use.

For those of you considering a diaper service, the rinsing, soaking and washing is done by them: that's what you are paying for. But for the home diaperer, let's take the process from the point after which baby is dry and clean and dressed with a fresh diaper, and you have a dirty one to deal with. Keep in mind that everybody does their laundry a little differently. Some don't rinse; other don't soak; others only soak soiled diapers and not wet ones; some store "dry," some store in a "wet" pre-soak. Eventually you will develop your own routine based on the types of diapers and covers you have, how often you wash, your lifestyle, and the kinds of cleaning agents you use. This is an amalgamation of some of the many ways I and others have laundered diapers in the past.

RINSING

Do you really have to soak or rinse?

There are definite anti-soaking advocates out there. And there is something to be said for doing it the way the diaper services do it.

After all, you don't rinse or soak those diapers, and somehow they come back to you each week perfectly white and beautifully sanitized.

The "non-soak, non-rinse" method, with my children, has worked well in the newborn phase (before solid food) because there really isn't much to soak anyway—breast-fed poop is kind of slimy and oozy and hard to dunk or rinse off. However, my children have all tended to have very wet, mushy poop, which does not shake off at all, smears all over everything and is the ultimate drudgery to soak off a diaper and the cover.

Let me tell you what we did during the time I wrote the first edition of *Diaper Changes*. I began washing my newborn's diapers, but kept the diaper service for my older child, who was in the midst of toilet training. That way I didn't have to rinse or dunk or deal with his worse-than-the-worst diapers in any way. I could barely shake anything off anyway, so I truly empathize with the lady down at the diaper service who had to open our bag every week!

Another way for parents to avoid rinsing would be to use liners, either reusable or throwaway, leave any residue on the diaper and just wait until wash day. If you have a baby or child whose poop just falls into the toilet, this method will work for you and you can thus avoid the soak/rinse drudgery. More power to you!

Rinsing wet diapers

I usually get some warm water going in either sink or bathtub and rinse wet (but unsoiled) diapers out there. Use your laundry room sink, if you have one! I'd probably set up my changing area there, if I had a toilet nearby. *(I am only talking about wet diapers! Soiled diapers must be rinsed in the toilet or bucket.)*

If they smell really bad I will soak them briefly with a little liquid soap (to cut the smell some, a cheap brand is okay) and then rinse off and chuck in the bucket. Then I wipe the sink carefully. Some of you may find the bathtub, or a separate "soaking" bucket a more aesthetically pleasing place to do this. (Be sure to empty it immediately lest someone get into it, or get a locking one.)

Some parents may find you don't want to bother rinsing wet diapers—which is fine as long as it doesn't stink up your house after a day or so! Some use two buckets, "wet" and "dirty" (soiled), so the soiled ones can get a little extra attention before adding the wet ones to the washing machine.

Laundry Time: Rinsing, Washing, Storing

Rinsing soiled diapers

If you are using throwaway liners, you can lift it up and throw it and the poop into the toilet. If you are using a reusable liner then just dunk that. You will probably still have stool on some of the diaper and even the cover. Depending on how bad it is, you may want to dunk the messy part of the diaper a bit before throwing it in the bucket. If you do not use a throwaway diaper liner then you will need to rinse your diaper or reusable liner as follows:

Take the diaper to the toilet and shake what you can into it, then flush. When you leave the diaper to soak you have to have an empty bowl, so be sure to flush. (If you use the Little Squirt water spray you avoid both soaking and dunking.) You may have to leave the diaper in there to soak a while (and if you are absent-minded like me I advise against it, because one of these days you'll forget it's there and go to the bathroom right on top of it—believe me) so if you can get most of the feces off by swishing it around a bit, do that. If you use a separate soaking bucket then you needn't worry about those things.

If you use a Diaper Duck, you can't avoid remembering there's a diaper in the toilet.

After swishing or dunking, flush again. Wring out well, or use the Diaper Duck or dip to wring out well. Hold on to the diaper because at least once I actually flushed a whole diaper because I didn't hold onto it. (Now you know I am a true airhead, and also why our septic system is all screwed up.) Then get the diaper into the bucket right away.

If you are a more fastidious sort, you could keep a pair of rubber gloves just for diaper dunking, and avoid getting poop on your hands at all.

To the bucket

The getting of this wet diaper to your diaper bucket is little tricky. You want to squeeze out as much water as possible, and then lift it (quickly!) to the bucket. Sometimes I take the lid off the diaper bucket, turn it around and carry the diaper on top of that. If your diaper bucket is next to the toilet, so much the better.

A locking diaper bucket

Please get a diaper bucket that locks shut! This will minimize the chances of the worst of all scenarios from happening, as babies have drowned in as little of two inches of water in a container. Plus it keeps curious babies from knocking your diaper bucket on the floor, slimy soak water running everywhere. (This is yet another reason why many people simply store soiled and wet diapers "dry," without any water in the bucket, until wash day.)

Keeping the diaper bucket from smelling

I most heartily advise rinsing diapers, no matter how little urine or stool is on them. This is your best deterrent to keeping your diaper bucket from smelling. The second deterrent would be a little water, mixed with some detergent or solvent in the bottom of your bucket, to kill more germs between loads.

If you like very natural things, Borax is one of those nice, old-fashioned products that happens to have little environmental impact and also deodorizes. You can use a little powdered laundry detergent. Or just a drop of Pine-Sol or Lysol or baking soda. This way, the first diapers you throw in there will basically be deodorized and degermed by the time the last one goes in and you are ready to do a load. This, plus rinsing before you throw them in, really cuts down on smell and keeps things sanitary. The effective DeoDisk will also mask any odor, too. Everything stays pretty clean and sanitary this way!

The diaper service

I love the convenience of a diaper service, but after a week of hot weather with unrinsed diapers sitting in there, even with the DeoDisk, they can start to reek. This is why I recommend rinsing if odor becomes a problem, especially in damp, yucky August, with flies around!

Rinsing covers

Perhaps you will need to rinse the cover in the sink. Use a little liquid soap, paste of powdered detergent, or an empty dish detergent bottle filled with liquid laundry detergent. Keep it nearby, and then just squeeze a little into the sink to rinse your covers as needed. Use something the manufacturer says you can use.

Especially for the wool covers, it's a good idea to scrub off any stool on the edges, because they function best when really clean, and this gets them so. If you do need to scrub a little soil off, no matter what cover you have, an old fingernail scrub brush works excellently! (Do mark that brush with an indelible ink pen so you don't end up using it on your fingers!)

Laundry Time: Rinsing, Washing, Storing

Now you have a pretty clean, wet diaper cover which you can keep in a small basket or container near or on top of your washer or dryer where it will be ready for the next wash. You can wash them with your regular laundry if you use cleaners in accordance with manufacturer's directions.

Between laundry loads

If it's going to be more than a day before the next laundry load, hang the cover or covers somewhere so they won't get mildewy. Some people who hand wash their covers use a carousel thing you hang in the bathtub. You could use your clothesline, or a radiator in the laundry room, or a hook in the shower. Since you have children, I can't imagine life without lots of laundry for you, so you'll be washing them soon enough!

Keeping covers easy

I hasten to remind you that one main point to consider when buying diaper covers is washability. I have found it a real pain to buy covers and find I could not wash them with my regular laundry, because Tide or whatever I use is too harsh. Then I ended up hand-washing them all the time which for me was an unnecessary burden when there are loads of easy-care covers around. If when you are looking through the catalogs and the washing advice says "machine (or hand) wash, mild detergent," call up and ask specifically what you can or cannot use on that particular cover. You may find that if you can't use your normal household detergent that it's just not worth it. I don't blame you. Go on to something else until you find the combination of washability, durability and breathability that suits you best.

No bleach

Whatever you do, *do not use chlorine bleach* on any kind of non-bleachable diaper cover (which virtually all are). It will ruin them instantly. Non-chlorine bleach, Biz, or other additives may be safe for your covers.

Thou shalt not procrastinate

Now you are done rinsing! Wonderful! My best advice in this area is not to procrastinate, because the smell and hassle only get worse as you leave the soiled diaper around on top of the bucket, or on your changing table, or in your ditty bag inside your diaper bag, making everything feel unsanitary.

WASHING

I really recommend washing diapers frequently, every two or three days at most. A small load every two days or so really gets cleaner than a larger one, and isn't as overwhelming to wash, dry, fold, and put away at a time. A few stories in this regard might encourage you as to why I have recommended this:

In the hot summer, flies can get into your diaper bucket. If you are careless with the lid this can happen particularly. And then what do you get? *Maggots.* Oh, I know this is disgusting, and revolting, and horrifying, and nauseating, but it happened to me both in the tropics of

Three natural cleaning aids: baking soda (deodorizes), borax (brightens and freshens), and vinegar (removes detergent residue and adjusts PH)

Hawaii and in the fertile Pennsylvania Dutch valley. And I was using both a diaper service and my own home laundry on these occasions.

A soak cycle

If you have soak water in your bucket, dump diapers in first and run one short spin cycle to get that slimy water out. Some parents will then use a long soak cycle with an additive like Borax to freshen and sanitize and really whiten the diapers. (This is a particularly good choice if you are using green cotton diapers and would like them as clean as bleach would get them, without the bleach.)

Throw in your reusable diaper bucket liner, if you use one. If you don't, you will need to briefly rinse out your bucket later (or use a kitchen garbage bag that fits and throw one away after each load). You may also wash your reusable wipes with your diaper load. Then wash diapers on hot with the detergent of your choice.

What kind of detergent?

Parents like anything from Ivory Snow, Dreft, and Tide, to alternative, low-impact cleaners like Ecover, Bio-Kleen, or Castile soap. Additives like Borax, baking soda, vinegar, a small amount of Lysol, or non-chlorine bleaches such as Biz are popular. You can add ¼ to ½ cup white vinegar in the rinse cycle to get rid of residue and lower your diaper's pH level (which discourages bacterial growth). You will have to see how your baby's skin tolerates both the type and quantity of cleaning agent or additive you use, and adjust your system as needed.

To bleach, or not to bleach

Although some companies say chlorine bleach is okay for diapers, I would not recommend it. I used to use it all the time, and the result was diapers that started ripping because the bleach literally ate the cotton away. So if you really want to use it because you like perfectly white diapers, I would say that if you'd rather not use a diaper service (they give you perfectly white ones every week) then use bleach sparingly, never on green cotton diapers, and not very often. And soak them in Biz or some alternative product between loads. Would bleaching every three months seem too long a spread?

Washing wool

Wool covers can be machine washed and hung to dry. Keep this in mind if you are planning to wash at odd times of the day. These cannot be machine dried, so you do need to allow extra drying time. Out in the sun would hasten things. Many mothers deal with covers before bed, so they are ready the next morning. Others wash each one as it becomes necessary, thus keeping them rotated. You can get one of those carousel clothespin dryers they sell at the store, or hang them on hooks in the bathroom. Most companies that sell wool diaper covers also offer special wool washes with lanolin to keep your covers water-resistant and very clean.

Double rinse

If your washer doesn't have a double rinse cycle, try to run them through an extra rinse if you can stand to remember it. The less detergent residue left in the diapers, the better. If you use liquid fabric softener on your diapers, you may find they become less absorbent as a film starts to develop over time, and this may irritate your baby's skin.

Are they clean?

Smell your diapers. They should have a pleasant, fresh smell. Sometimes they get this unpleasant, old "poop-stink" smell, even after washing. This means they need another cleaning. When this happens I just run them through again, with some baking soda, Borax, or vinegar. Make sure you don't put too many diapers in at a time, and make sure you use enough detergent. Hey, the diaper services use thirteen washes and rinses, so if you have to wash them again, no big deal. You want clean, fresh diapers!

DRYING: DRYER AND CLOTHESLINE

When you dry in the dryer, do not use fabric softener sheets (on diapers or diaper covers), because they cause a film to develop, hindering absorption. Heavier and thicker diapers require longer drying times.

If you dry on a clothesline, the overlap technique saves space as well as clothespins. Start pinning the left side of one diaper, and before you pin the right side of that diaper, get another diaper and pin its left side underneath the first diaper's right side, so they overlap. And on and on. After they are dry, you can shake them and pull them a little to soften, or use your dryer for a couple of minutes.

overlap technique

What about a laundromat? The dry diaper method

Yes, it can be done! This is what I call the "dry diaper" method, and is also useful in very hot, fly-prone weather, when you'd rather not have a bucket full of diaper stuff sitting around for any length of time.

Here's how to do it

With a bucket that has a locking lid (since it's pretty full), fill pail with very hot water and a spoonful of Borax or other additive to make a soaking solution. Keep this far away from little, curious children. If the idea of a lot of water scares you, you can simply soak a few diapers at a time in less water and follow same method—only there won't be a six-hour soak. Dunk off any large fecal masses into toilet. Soak diapers in the bucket about six hours, or overnight and deal with in the A.M.

In the morning, rinse and squeeze diapers damp dry. Then dump out and rinse your bucket. Leave these pre-washed, fully soaked diapers to dry out—a day's worth at a time, on a small clothes rack near your window (for apartment dwellers) or one resting in your bathtub. Sunlight helps kill germs and deodorize. In a day you will have a dry, nice pile which you can collect in a bag or grocery cart until wash day.

In a large commercial machine you can get fifty diapers in at a time—about six days worth or so. You can wash more often if you need to by bringing a smaller load to the laundromat at a time.

On laundry day, instead of lugging an unbearable load of wet, soggy, smelly, embarrassing diapers to the laundromat, you bring your *dry*, neat, halfway clean, pre-soaked bundle. Use ½ cup vinegar in the final rinse to adjust the pH and deodorize.

Hand wash and line dry diaper covers and keep reusing them until wash day when you can give your supply a good cleaning with one of your regular commercial laundry loads.

I tried the dry diaper method this summer, in the heat of fly and maggot season. This was so much better than dealing with the nastiness summer can bring to diapering.

STORING

When, at the end of your endeavors, you have a nice pile of clean, sweet diapers, and a supply of covers ready for another round of use, then what? Some mothers fold flat diapers (and even prefolds) in the shape they like them to be so they are ready for the next round of changes with little effort. Others just drop everything into a pretty wicker laundry basket near your changing area and keep everything unfolded but easily accessible. Fold and store the best way that makes diapering pleasant and convenient for you.

One final point: stains vs. clean

You know, this is an imperfect world, and children's clothes are the hardest to keep clean and from getting stained. If the diaper is clean—deodorized, sanitized, and nice-smelling—does it really matter if it has some stains on it? Many parents are going for green (unbleached) cotton as a way to say "no" to a perfectly white world where nothing gets or stays dirty. (Stains just blend in to the off-white fabric also.)

For a long time I used slightly stained diapers my diaper service could no longer use, because for them they *must* be perfect. I bought them cheap, and got more stains on them from my own children. So what? They still did the same great job, and nobody really bothered to inspect the whiteness or absence of stains on my diapers! So think about it.

DIAPER CHANGES

You'll get used to it!

Has it all sounded overwhelming to you, a huge laborious process, a real pain in the neck? The descriptions sound a little that way, but try to describe how to make a sandwich, or tying your shoes, and even that can sound complicated. It's really no different than brushing your teeth; it's a simple thing that you have to do that you get used to doing. I encourage those of you who haven't tried cloth before, to go ahead, give it a try. You might wish to "break in" with a diaper service for a few months—though I encourage you to stick with one if it suits you! Or get some samples from a couple of diaper companies, if you plan to wash at home, so you can find a system which works for you and your family.

No matter what

We have to deal with urine and feces no matter what, with sights and smells no matter what. Your baby is a baby and will need this attention for the next two and a half years or so. But when you combine this necessary chore with a whole lot of love and gratitude, it's not as bad as all of that!

The next chapter of *Diaper Changes* deals with setting up your own home diapering system—and how to take it with you when you need to.

CHAPTER 9

Staying Home and Going Out with Diapers

Diapering at home

Where and how to set up your home diapering system? Room size, fixture placement, furniture, even your height make a difference in your choices. Basically, if you can change baby near where you dunk or throw your diapers, good. Have you got a bathroom large enough? Then you could dress baby afterward in the bedroom or wherever you keep his clothes. You won't have to walk around the house carrying soiled diapers this way.

But for those of us with small bathrooms, we do have to carry the diaper from the changing area to the toilet. Unless you use throwaway wipes or a wipe warmer, you'll have to wet a washcloth in the bathroom before changing baby in your bedroom or wherever. That's two trips to the bathroom and back. If you change baby on the bathroom floor (and keep items nearby, or on a shelf or whatever and not use a changing table), you save a trip. So look around your house and see where you can get the most done with the least effort. You've got a lot of other things to do in a day!

If you use a diaper service, however, you could get by with keeping everything in the bedroom, since for the most part you do not need to rinse. I would still shake off what I could into the toilet if possible. You can't really "shake" newborn, breast-fed stool, so for the first few months with a service you might have it easy in your bedroom. Use a wipe warmer, or throwaways (low chemical ones, please!).

Look at my charts for ideas on how to set up your changing area. I think shelves are wonderful because it enables you to remain upright most of the time and not have to bend into a drawer. It keeps everything where you can see it and away from baby's reach. Use the ideas as a springboard to design something to meet your own particular needs.

You could keep your diaper bag on the shelf, stocked, and just work out of it; or keep a second inventory on your shelves at all times. Those hanging diaper holders are either chintzy or lovely; I made one 6 years ago which is still going strong. See if one would work for you. They don't hold all that many diapers.

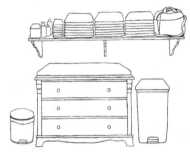 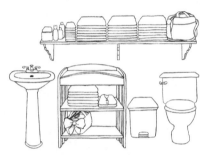

A bedroom changing area   A bathroom changing area

Going on an outing

I am basically addressing the mother at home with her young baby, but those of you working outside the home can apply this advice to off-days or weekends.

If you can possibly manage it, do try to get out every day with your baby. It makes the house really nice to come home to, clears you head, and releases tension from the routine and cyclical nature of child care and household duties. Especially if you tidy up before going out, it's a relief to get back home.

Many diaper bags are designed with snaps which make them easy to hang on your stroller. Some stroller bags can be used in place of a diaper bag (they'd stay put on the stroller), depending on what you plan to carry. Whatever you do, it is important to be well-prepared for any length outing. This improves the quality of the endeavor tremendously.

Staying Home and Going Out with Diapers

What to take

Rule of thumb number one—*always carry at least one diaper and a spare.* One diaper usually goes for two hours, so even for the shortest trip, carry a diaper, and a spare, in case a big mess occurs or you end up being out longer than expected. A spare cover, if you are using cloth, is also wise. You may wish to purchase a "little tripper" or other short trip-type diaper bag for these quick jaunts, or use a large purse you may already have.

The Shortest Trip
- *One or two diapers*
- *Wipes*
- *Ditty bag*

For an average trip, you may want to include extras that will keep you and baby busy, feed you both, and keep things clean. Stock your diaper bag well and your trip will be easy!

The Average Trip
- *One diaper for every two hours expected to be out, plus one spare, or one disposable for every two hours*
- *One cover for every 2 to 3 diapers*
- *Ditty bag(s)*
- *Wipes, in container or Ziploc bag* (throwaway or reusable)
- *Snacks* (for you, and baby if old enough)
- *Drinks* (in tight, non-spillable containers)
- *Reading and writing material* (in case baby falls asleep in the park or you have time to kill waiting for lunch at the mall)
- *Toys and books* (small enough and age appropriate)
- *Powders, ointments, or whatever you like to use* (travel sizes)
- *Baby nail clipper* (best time to clip is when baby's asleep)
- *Change of clothes* (almost always comes in handy)
- *Bibs and washcloths* (keeps things sane)
- *Bottles* (if you use them. There's a lot of paraphernalia out there but I never used them)
- *Stain stick* (treat stains on baby's clothes right away)
- *Brush, and extra clips or rubber bands*
- *Hat, sweater, jacket as needed*
- *Baby sunscreen as needed*
- *Your wallet, checkbook, keys and other personal items*

Now you know why a decent, durable diaper bag is important! Believe me, it somehow all fits in there and you wonder how you did it!

The Extended Trip

Unless you know you will have a place you can wash your diapers, I would say that the extended trip is the one real place where a disposable diaper makes sense. I have lugged around several dozen cloth diapers, and then bags of soiled ones, and I do think a disposable is made for a real trip. Realize that I have used and do use cloth diapers virtually all other times in existence!

For diehard cloth users, try using the thin, flat gauze diapers for your extended trip. You can fold them how you like and then rinse them in the hotel or campground toilet or hand wash in the sink. These will air-dry quickly and are thin enough to pack very tightly. Use one-gallon Ziploc bags or ditty bags, handy both for the clean and soiled diapers. Know which bags are for what!

Use the guidelines for the average trip as a basis for planning long-term packing. I like to *pack baby's extra stuff in a separate bag or suitcase,* and then keep the diaper bag handy for the car or whatever, filled basically like an ordinary day.

You forgot your wipes?

Here's how to improvise. Paper towels wetted with a little soap from the ladies room of the nearest restaurant will work. So will toilet paper, though not as easily. In a real pinch use one of your spare diapers—or ask the lady near you at the park!

Going for a ride

Especially on car trips, do stop every couple of hours to let baby's bottom air out a little. You will probably do this to nurse or change him anyway. Sitting for long periods in the same position can lead to compromised circulation, urine irritation, and pressure which leads to redness and rash. For very new babies a kind of flat crib car seat would solve this circulation problem as baby lies flat.

How to change baby in gross public bathrooms

It has amazed me the level of funk, filth, grunge, and disgustingness out there at ye local gas station, and even some restaurants. You have to wonder what the kitchens are like! I'd just as soon go back to the car and change baby there. Fortunately, family-oriented places are starting to come of age regarding parents' needs, and many now have a pull-down, ironing board-type thing you would use to change baby. I would *never, never, ever* change baby on a public bathroom floor (or any public floor) no matter what. Put baby on your lap, sitting on the toilet, if you have to. Change them in the stroller. But please, keep your precious bundle away from that nasty grossness, please! If you must change baby on a counter or sink area or even a changing station, do put your changing pad underneath—and be sure to wash it when you get home. An old blanket would be great for situations like this!

I would love to see clean, hospitable places for mothers and babies, a higher level of awareness of the potential for disease and contamination in unclean places we all must frequent. It sure never feels clean coming out of one of "those" bathrooms, if you know what I mean!

The final chapter of *Diaper Changes* is all about diapering creatively—using fabric, talent, and time to make anything from diapers to covers to a matching layette set. Come and join me in the world of textiles and ingenuity!

Chapter 10

Make Your Own

This last chapter of *Diaper Changes* is especially dear to my heart because I love homemade things and enjoy my avocation as seamstress. When it comes to baby items, hardly anything is treasured more than a hand-made garment or useful article for the new little one. Out of all the gifts I have received for my children over the years, the ones I have hung on to are the crocheted pastel blanket from my dear friend, the hand-knotted flannel blanket from my Grandma, my own hand-blocked crib quilt, the bunting and saques and diaper holder I whipped up during pregnancies. Perhaps the ideas for diapering products here will inspire you to coordinate other layette or baby items, like receiving blankets, diaper holders, bumper pads and ruffles, curtains, clothing. We shall explore making your own flat, prefold, and fitted diapers, soakers, wool felt covers with Velcro, changing pads, wipes, and ditty bags.

Theresa's homemade blue wool felt diaper cover

The fabric store! The place where ideas and the potential to make them a reality meet. My creativity flourishes in that colorful haven of textiles, hues, densities, and uses. In making diapering products you want to be looking out for fabrics such as flannel, birdseye, and terrycloth for diapers, wool, waterproof nylons, polyesters, or Ultrex for covers, strong woven cottons for changing pads, waterproof fabrics for ditty bags.

homemade fitted diaper

Ultrex tie-on cover

DIAPER CHANGES

One of my fullest joys is to make soft, warm things for my children. I have made sets of wool diaper covers, quilts, hats, buntings, pants, blouses, jumpers, bloomers, slips, dresses, and more. As you know, I adore natural fibers, and a child wrapped in something nice to touch makes the touching all the more pleasant!

I go for bargains. I'd about fall apart if, say, I saw a bolt of flannel for fifty cents or a dollar a yard! Yes! Make diapers! And when I did get the wool felt for my diaper covers, it was a remnant bolt as well.

So periodically check your stores for rare things like wool felt or waterproof nylon. Sources for Ultrex (a Gore-Tex type fabric) are also in Appendix B. Buy that bolt or remnant and keep on hand to make gifts for your next expectant friend or relative—or yourself.

With notions, I have found things like Velcro cheaply when on sale. I even took the soft Velcro parts from old wool covers that shrunk and reused them in my new covers. Stock up on ¼" or ⅜" elastic for legs and ½" to ¾" for waistbands. You could even use a sturdy drawstring for the waist, if you are earthier than I am!

The beauty of "homemade" is in the serendipity of it. You'll never know what you'll find! How do you like that layered, kind of coordinated mismatching of the "country look"? Checks with stripes with calicos. Nice for baby stuff, too—colorful print flannel for diapers, Ultrex or wool covers in assorted colors, bright nylon changing pads. An expansion of the time-honored "what have I in my hand" philosophy: using what you have in your home, in the attic, from what friends give you, what you find on sale or at a yard sale, to make many of the common things you need. It's kind of an adventure, pulling things out and seeing how you can use—or reuse them. You become more content with what you have, and a whole lot more inventive.

I am writing to those of you with some sewing experience. Please consult someone with sewing knowledge or sewing manuals should you need basic guidance for these projects.

Suggested sizes for making diapers

There's a lot of room for variety here. If you end up cutting and folding and stitching your diapers differently than I suggest here, fine. These are some guidelines you could follow.

Flat diapers can range from a 27" square to a rectangle 18" × 36" to 18" × 45".

Regular prefolds may be found in any of the following dimensions: 15" × 18", 13" × 18", 14" × 18", 14" × 17", 14" × 20", 14" × 21", 15" × 22", 16" × 21".

Newborn size prefolds can run 10" × 14", 12" × 16", 11" × 14". For the following guidelines I list by the width of fabric and discuss flat, prefold, and newborn size diapers for each. *All dimensions are approximate and based on one yard of fabric before washing and shrinking.* Flat diapers are sized before hemming.

Diapers from different widths (1 yard length)

27"

Can make a flat diaper 27" square. If you buy 3 yards you will get four 27" square diapers exactly. You could make two prefolds by cutting two pieces 27" × 18". Folded in half will yield a two-layer diaper 13½" × 18". An inner terry layer would be desirable.

You could get four two-layer newborn sized diapers 9" × 13½", but this is kind of small.

36"

You can make two flat diapers 18" × 36". Fold these to make two three-layer prefolds 12" × 18".

You could make two two-layer newborn diapers 9" × 12" but this is also kind of small.

45"

Can yield two flat diapers 18" × 45". Can make four two-layer prefolds 11" × 18". Add inner terry layer if desired. Can also make 2 thicker prefolds 13" × 18" with extra center panel if folded this way: fold in thirds, first left side in 13", then right side in only 10" instead of the whole 13". Then fold the extra material back over to the right another 5", then to the left the remaining 5". Pin to secure center panel. Stitch either side of panel, bind top and bottom as explained below.

Can make four 2-layer newborn diapers with center padding approximately 11" × 14". Cut 4 pieces 22½" × 18". Fold in half. Cut off the extra 4 inches and center inside the folded diaper. Pin to secure. Straight stitch either side of panel to secure. Finish as explained below.

DIAPER CHANGES

60"

This size will yield four two-layer prefolds 18" × 15". Cut four pieces 30" × 18" and then fold in half. You could also make two three-layer prefolds 14" × 20". To do this you would cut the 18" side down to a more usable 14" and turn diaper so the 20" side is now vertical. Use the extra 4" as a center padding as described above.

Newborn-sized prefolds

To make newborn-sized prefolds, cut four pieces 30" × 18". Cut 18" side to 14" and use extra 4" as center padding as described above. Will yield four three-layer prefolds 10" × 14" with center padding.

Finishing flat diapers

Cut material to size. Fold ¼", then ¼" again on each side of diaper. Sew straight stitch seam around the entire perimeter to finish.

Finishing prefold diapers

You will either have a raw edge or the selvage(s) exposed along the length of the diaper after folding. Fold the diaper so that selvage edge or raw edge lies between the center of the diaper and the folded outer edge. Look at any prefold to use as a guide. Turn raw edge under ¼" or so, if you have one, to avoid an unfinished seam on the length of the diaper. Add inner layer(s) of terry or flannel during folding if desired. Pin all layers. Sew straight seam over the selvage or folded raw edge on the one side of the diaper, and another seam exactly like it on the other side of the diaper to be even and secure all layers. Trim top and bottom of diaper if needed. Straight stitch top and bottom of diaper ⅜" from raw edge. Then go back serge top and bottom raw edges to bind, or use a long, narrow zigzag stitch to bind the raw edges.

It took me exactly five minutes to cut, fold, pin and sew a prefold diaper, and I'm not that fast! These will go quickly for you and you could make a dozen diapers in an hour or so.

Preshrink diaper fabric if you are using an inner terry layer that has already been washed (like an old towel). This way the outer fabric won't over-shrink and pucker over the toweling. Since your material will be a little smaller after shrinking, keep that in mind if using my dimensions for making diapers.

Another way

Another way to make diapers would be to cut two outer layers of fabric to your finished desired size, and then add any inner panels or layers as desired. Pin all layers and finish as described above by straight stitching the entire perimeter and then by serging or zigzagging the entire outer edge.

Fitted and contour diapers

Patterns are available to make fitted diapers with or without Velcro. You could use snaps instead, but if you plan to use a snug-fitting diaper cover you might do well to leave off both snaps and Velcro. The best use for a fitted diaper with Velcro would be with any pull-on cover or wool soakers, as these covers tend to fit loosely.

You could buy a sample contour diaper and make your own pattern from it. One layer of flannel and one layer of thick terry work well for this style of diaper. Finish contour by running straight seam ⅜" from outer edge along entire perimeter, then binding entire edge with serging or zigzag as described above.

Diaper liners

If you were to cut a single layer of flannel or other soft cloth to a finished size of 6" × 14", this would serve as a nice reusable diaper liner. Serge edges of piece of cloth cut to size, or add ½" all around, turn under twice, and zigzag entire perimeter.

Even a washcloth could work as a reusable diaper liner.

On the price per homemade diaper

Keep in mind how much each diaper is going to cost you, based on the price of fabric per yard. 60" fabric will yield two three-layer prefolds approximately 20" × 15" with extra center material. 45" fabric will yield two two-layer prefolds about 22" × 15". For newborn diapers you could get four three-layer diapers 10" × 14" per 60" yard, or four two-layer diapers per 45" yard. Added terry or flannel layers will make them as thick as you like.

So if you miraculously got flannel at $1 or $2 a yard, you could make your own prefolds for 50¢ to $1 a piece. If you end up spending more than $1.50 per diaper I wouldn't bother, unless you have fabric laying around or you get it for free. Good commercial prefolds start at about $2 apiece, so what's the sense of making them for as much, unless you love to sew anyway or want to use a particular fabric?

Fitted diapers, however, and some contours tend to be quite a bit more expensive than prefolds, so making these yourself will generally be a bargain. For example, a fitted diaper runs $3 to $6 each, or even as high as $8 to $9 each. The Quick-Sew fitted diaper pattern (see diaper fabric and pattern resources below) requires ¾ to 1¼ yards of 45" fabric, depending on size, to make a fitted diaper. Similarly, the Baby Softwear fitted diaper pattern requires 5.2 meters to make six diapers (a little over a yard apiece). If your flannel or other diaper fabric is more than 3 or 4 dollars a yard, it may not be worth it to you. These figures give you a ballpark idea of costs involved.

For your inner terry layers, nothing could work better than old terry towels, hand towels, or even washcloths. If you plan to bleach your diapers, stay away from colored terry. The old terry is usually on the inside where no one can see it, so who cares what it looks like?

On the price of homemade diaper covers

This will depend on the pattern you use and how many layers you choose to include. The very best fabric available to make waterproof diaper covers that breathe is Ultrex, which runs $8.25 to $8.50 a yard. Don't gasp! A very simple, tie-on diaper pattern only uses ⅛ of a yard of Ultrex per cover, so it costs you about a dollar a piece to make covers this way (see diaper resources below). A more traditional cover with Velcro will require ½ to ⅝ of a yard of Ultrex per cover, which is still pretty good—a decent, breathable cover for about $4 apiece. If you are making a wool felt Velcro cover, and your wool costs $9 a yard, you will still be making out well, as wool Velcro covers run $16 to $24 apiece! If you choose to add an outer flannel layer for Ultrex covers, the cost will increase, but you really don't need any. Just adapt the pattern for a single layer, and making diaper covers is easy!

Wool pull-on soakers from old sweaters

Yes, people really do this. What you need are old, discarded, or donated 100% wool sweaters. Any you shrunk by accident would be great for this project. Do preshrink any others by washing and drying a couple of times on hot to start. Then the wool will be thick, felt-like, and the right density for a diaper cover.

Use an existing pair of pull-ons, or even a pair of full-fitting girls panties to form the basis of your soaker pattern. This is a very loose medium so nothing need be exact by any means. Trace the item onto newsprint or freezer paper. Add 1" all the way around for seams. The back and the front will be about the same so you'll cut two pieces from the one pattern piece.

Lay your pattern on the sweater so the bottom of the sweater (with its nice, finished edge) is now the top part of the soaker and will form the waistband. If you cut off the arms of the sweater first it will make cutting and dealing easier. Use the arms as leg warmers for baby. Pin pattern and cut two pieces.

Sew sides and crotch, then leg and waist casings to fit size elastic you are using. Size elastic to be snug but not too tight. Insert elastic through casings, tack, and finish casings as for any other leg or waistband.

What you did was make a pair of wool underpants! That's what a soaker really is. Then you pin your old-fashioned diapers underneath or use fitted snap or Velcro diapers.

If you have a shrunken wool felt blanket, save it and make Velcro diaper covers. Leave off the Velcro if you choose and just pin where the Velcro would be (people have done that).

If you knit, make soakers using a panties or bloomers pattern and 100% virgin wool yarn. Make large to allow for shrinkage. See appendix for a knitted soaker pattern.

Making pull-on pants

Use Ultrex fabric. Cut apart an old pull-on pant at the side seams. You will have one piece of material which you can use for a pattern. Add ½" for seams. Pin and cut. Sew casings for legs and run ⅜" elastic cut to size for each leg. Tack all ends. Sew side seams. Finish by making casing for waist and running elastic through to fit.

Making a ditty bag

Use Ultrex, waterproof poly, waterproof nylon, or vinyl.

The beauty of making these yourself is you can make whatever size suits you. An average bag is a finished 9" × 12" but for longer trips I like them bigger (12" × 16"). Add ½" for seams and 2" on top to fold under for casing. Leave casing open on both sides and run a thick, sturdy nylon cord through. Insert both loose ends through a toggle. Tie ends beyond toggle to secure.

Making a changing pad

Cut two pieces of outer fabric for a finished size 12" × 22" or so. Add inner terry layer if desired. Pin all layers. Quilt fabric by running a straight stitch evenly placed three or four times in both directions to secure layers and look decorative. Add seam binding to entire perimeter. Secure binding by a decorative zigzag through all layers.

If you had two old (or new) hand towels the same size, these would make a fine changing pad. You wouldn't need an inner layer, just quilt and add seam binding.

Making your own baby wipes

This is the paper towel method. Obtain an old round throwaway tub (the kind with the slit in the top that the wipes are pulled through). Cut a paper towel roll in half. Use only heavy, high-quality towels. Remove cardboard tube and place inside tub. Make a mixture of 2 to 3 cups water, 2 to 3 tablespoons shampoo, baby castile soap or baby bath, and 1 to 2 tablespoons of olive oil, calendula oil or other baby oil. Mix and pour over roll. After liquid is absorbed, pull toweling from center of roll and through the slit on top of tub.

Another way to do this would be to buy the half-size paper towels, make them into a stack, place in ½-pint size freezer bag, and pour a portion of liquid over them. Zip and take along. Or carry a small bottle of liquid, dry toweling, and wet as needed.

Reusable baby wipes the cheap way

Buy the thin, cheap terry washcloths in the 10- or 12-pack at Wal-Mart for under five bucks, or check your local bargain store. Buy white if you bleach and off-white if you don't. Then save soap scraps with some water in an empty liquid soap dispenser and have liquid soap for nothing. Liquid baby castile would also work very well in such a dispenser. The thin terry washcloths work better than thick, expensive ones, so look at your local five-and-dime next time and see what they have.

Another idea is to cut up an old terry towel into comfortable 5" squares. Serge edges if you like, but terry doesn't really run.

Diaper bucket for a dollar

I really did use one of these for a while. Get a large food-grade bucket from a bakery, one with a lid that's easy to open (some are harder than others—check first). Make sure it has a metal handle. They'll either give it to you or charge you a dollar. Take it home, wash it out well, and write *Diapers Only, No Food* with indelible ink on the lid and on the bucket.

This bucket will hold two to three days worth of diapers or more, depending on size. Cover with wallpaper or contact if you feel especially creative. Try a stick-on room freshener in the lid in lieu of a DeoDisk.

Please see Appendix B which includes sources for diaper patterns and hard-to-find items like Ultrex, washable waterproof nylon, seam sealer, bleachable elastic, and organic and green cotton by the yard. With this mini-resource guide you should be able to make some great diapers and diaper covers!

On to the Company and Resource Guide!

The Company and Resource Guide

This is in many ways the meat and potatoes of this book. It is here that you will find the differences in price, quality, construction, and style between the brands each company carries.

What has changed since the Second Edition

In the last five years our family went from four children to six, the last of whom, at two and a half years of age, is at the tail end of toilet training as of this writing. She is just in training pants and padded underpants during the day and doing great. I never thought the day would come for me that I would neither be pregnant, nursing a baby, or changing any diapers (usually all of them at once), but after thirteen incredible years, that time has come for me.

The outside diapering world has changed, too. Whereas once a company might have heavily relied on a catalog to advertise and sell merchandise, now the Internet has overwhelmed and consumed us all; for most of us it is now part of our daily lives, along with other forms of electronic media with which we have lived for so long.

I therefore made a decision to exclude most companies that do not have a website for you to go to. The exceptions are those that sell some very unusual or exclusive items that would not be possible to obtain through the Internet. A catalog is indeed nice to have; but when you are in a rush, or need something soon, or enjoy shopping online, the wait of ordering and receiving a catalog becomes outmoded.

What I have also noticed is a growing number of home-based businesses attempting to sell diapering products, virtually saturating the internet market. I wonder if this does not come from some romantic notion of the stay-at-home mom who works from home while nursing a baby or two at the computer (perhaps from having read my company reviews in previous editions of *Diaper Changes!*). What I have also noticed is how quickly these operations rise and fall. Many of them are gone in less than six months—probably because the realities of running a business, whether from home or not—become overwhelming to many newbies. This sort of situation puts new parents like you at a disadvantage. *Can I trust this fly-by-night operation I am ordering from? Will I get what I ordered on time? Do they have an honest returns policy? Can I expect knowledgeable customer service? Will they actually be in business next week?*

It is for this reason that I have only included in this new edition of the resource guide the companies that existed in the second edition. These companies have been in business at least five years—some as many as twenty years. There is much to indicate that they will be around in years to come and not rise and fall with the next wave of diapering fanatcism. There are many other little start-up operations out there and I am aware of them; but I am not doing you any favors by including them here.

And on the issue of fanaticism, another thing I have noticed in the last five years is how very important the issue of diapering has become to those who are clothing and style-conscious. I have read message boards on various websites about moms comparing diaper covers and diapers with one another: *"I have my 2-wk old in Bookie-Snoos"* . . . *"My son wears only Lovie Dumps"* . . . *"My twins wouldn't be caught dead in anything but matching Diapie-Doos"* You get the idea. Since when is diapering a social and fashion statement? Please beware when you get into the Internet on this subject that the world seems to get smaller as the house gets bigger—moms who don't get out much or are having big changes in their lives with new babies like to make powerful judgements on Internet chat rooms about products and diaper companies as well. Some of it gets very petty and small-minded—curious for women who by and large are well-educated, affluent, and informed! Limit your time at these sites, or stay away entirely, and keep your minds and hearts focused where they should be—on your baby and your family, diapering in the best way that you can afford and enjoy, being the best mom or dad you can be. Leave gossip and small talk to soap operas!

Changes to the Third Edition of the Resource Guide

The Resource Guide has proven to be what I intended it to be: a way for moms to quickly get a handle on the diapering/parenting world and what products are available to them. I have continued previous aspects and improved the Resource Guide in this third edition with the following features:

- All current websites, e-mail, fax numbers, and toll-free numbers, where available, are included and updated, along with any name changes in the company. Websites are listed in bold and e-mail addresses are listed in italics. Some companies have been renamed or acquired by another company, and I mention this when warranted.
- Companies which have gone out of business since the second edition are deleted. I have made a conscious decision to include only those companies that have been around since the first and second editions. Too many short-lived companies exist that fail to measure up to the standard required for a book with shelf life, and I have not included them; if you wish to find the latest company (which in my experience has a life of about six months to a year), then the Internet sites I list at the conclusion of the Resource Guide will have plenty of them for you too choose from. I do believe, however, that I have included more than an ample supply of reliable, good businesses—a special community of companies—with excellent, time-tested products for you to choose from here.
- The pricing section at the end of each company review has been changed to make it easier to read. Brand names are in bold, followed by the products made by that brand. That way if you are, say, looking to compare the prices of Bumkins all-in-ones among several companies, you can find the Bumkins listing among the others offered by those catalogs quickly. I have basically stuck to diaper and cover prices only.
- I have included information about the individual companies, such as statements from the owners, company philosophy, special services or products offered and distinguishing features.
- A separate Diapers and Covers Review section, which reviews all in one place some some of the more popular diapering products under the name of the manufacturer. This way there is virtually no repetition in the company reviews. Previously I had to say the

same thing many times if a certain product was carried by many companies. If a company has a unique or exclusive offering, it is reviewed within that company review.

- A separate extra resource website appendix, listing the better websites related to diapering and reviews of the sites for your convenience.

How this works

I would suggest the following course: read through all the diaper and cover reviews first. Then you can either read through the entire Resource Guide or read just under the company reviews that have the kind of product or products you are looking for. You can also use the product index to find sources for diapers, covers, and accessories as well—but here the products will be listed by type and not by brand name.

The Product Index

Are you looking for organic diapers, or wool pull-on soakers, or bed pads, or perhaps natural cleaning agents? The product index will give you a list of who carries any specific type of diaper, or diaper cover, or accessory available in our list of companies. Each company carrying the product you are investigating will be listed underneath, with the page number to turn to. This way you can compare prices as well as differences within a certain product category.

From here it would be a matter of ordering catalogs from those companies (or much better yet, save resources and visit their websites if possible), comparing prices, and perhaps ordering a sample of each to find out which one you like. Some companies offer sample sets, so if you can narrow your search down you might find you'll only need to order samples from one or two companies.

If you are looking for a product carried by many companies—like the ubiquitous diaper service quality prefold—consider several things. You want excellent, attentive customer service. When you order your catalogs, who seems genuinely interested in you, your baby, your personal diapering situation? You may get your products a little cheaper from somebody else, but make your whole diapering experience pleasant by buying from a company with excellent customer service, and not just the bottom line dollar. Also consider the other diaper-related items they carry, or the other types of products they carry.

This may help you choose one company over another. For instance, if you were planning on getting organic bedding anyway, why not combine your diapering purchase with a company offering the kind of bedding you were looking for, and save some money on postage this way?

So many companies, you might say! Well, this is a good sign that the interest in cloth diapering has widened and companies have responded to the need with better and more innovative products. But don't let all the names throw you off—if you stick to my basic definitions you will fare okay. And you will undoubtedly find something else—like herbal remedies, organic baby clothes, parenting books, or wooden toys—that you may (or may not) have been looking for!

About mail order and the Internet

You usually (almost always) cannot find interesting, high-quality diaper-related items in retail stores, so getting them through the mail or online is the way to go. Do figure in postage costs when making price comparisons. Remember—you usually only pay sales tax if the company you are ordering from is located, or has branches, in your state. This goes for online ordering as well. (This may change in the future, if certain legislation on the table is passed into law that will require sales tax on all mail-order/Internet purchases, in or out of state). So at least for now, you save a little, and pay a little. Many companies offer free shipping over a certain dollar amount of purchase, or if you buy a certain number of items. And once you're on somebody's list, you'll be surely getting more and more catalogs (unless you request otherwise) where that came from!

About prices

The prices given here are not to be taken as permanent, unchanging, gospel, or forever. Prices are bound to go up, rather than down. Still, sales and closeouts do happen. When you actually get a catalog in your hands you may find that your prices are the same, lower, or higher than what is presented in the Resource Guide. Generally, it will be relatively close to what I have given you.

Also note that often in the pricing section what is listed after a product is range of prices—which means the prices for several sizes are listed together. The smaller sizes are the cheaper end of the price range and the higher prices are the larger or perhaps toddler sizes.

Buying Canadian

Americans buying Canadian products benefit from a very favorable exchange rate—which means you pay about 30 percent less than the price listed in a Canadian catalog. The exchange rate is calculated automatically by your credit card company or bank. Postage costs of a few dollars will be added to the regular postage and handling fee. I think you will be pleased with what the exchange rate will do to a lot of the prices for products sold by companies from Canada.

About small/home-based businesses

Quite a number of the companies listed in the Resource Guide are family-run, or more likely, mother-run businesses, perhaps out of a spare bedroom, with inventory in the basement or garage. In between are companies with perhaps a retail store and mail-order, and a staff of a few (friends, family, or others). Then there are, of course, a few multimillion dollar companies with numerous staff, warehouses, and huge inventory. Some of the former grow to become the latter, in time. On the way there, it can be a real challenge for the "mompreneur," or mother running a business from her home. She is juggling, perhaps, being pregnant, nursing a little baby, chasing a busy toddler or two, perhaps homeschooling, dealing with older children, and managing her household—in addition to taking your order, answering your questions, giving her expert advice and wisdom, sending catalogs, working on computer, packing your order, getting to the post office—it can be a real challenge! She is the order department; the customer service department; the advertising department; the clerk; the accountant; the buyer; the designer; the secretary; the gofer. And yet, you will not find better people equipped to really help you with your baby/ diapering/parenting questions. These are not just telephone sales reps; these are the living, breathing reality you are entering into. I can't think of better companies to patronize if you are looking for personal, attentive service and some of the best diapering/baby/children's products available anywhere. I would take an experienced mom's advice and help—even if I have to wait for a return call—over a mere order-taker any day.

But sometimes the voice mail will take your call—because mom must go grocery shopping or is putting baby down for a nap. Sometimes your order may take a day longer to get to you than you expected—because she had a bad day toilet training her toddler or she has morning sickness or perhaps the house just needed a good cleaning. It is impossible to do everything at once. So understand that behind the nice catalog you just got or the beautiful website you just visited is very likely a very busy mom, doing many things, working as hard and as fast as she can. And don't wait for the last minute—like the week before your due date (or even when labor begins, as some moms have!)—to order your diapers. Give all this some thought and time beforehand if you possibly can. Then you can best enjoy shopping and the benefits of ordering through of the excellent home-based businesses I present to you.

Returns

Most companies do not offer returns on products that have been used, soiled, or washed. After all, they can't resell it, even if you don't like it. The best thing to do is narrow your search to three or four companies that seem to have what you want, order their catalogs, and then order samples which you can try at a small cost. The worst thing to do is order two or three or four dozen of any diaper, wash them all, and then expect the company to take them back if they are not what you are looking for. Read their returns policy carefully, and be respectful of what limitations are given you.

Another note

Businesses, especially small, home-run ones, of which many diapering companies consist, often have highly changeable inventories, due to a good deal on a sell-out of something, trade problems overseas, employees who hand-craft items having another baby, or what have you. Often you will find even in a current catalog that something you were eagerly awaiting is discontinued, out-of-stock, or replaced by something else. Whole companies rise up and disappear at once (although I have made an effort to only include companies who are not likely to do so!). This happens all the time and has to be expected.

What I have most earnestly endeavored is to keep my company product descriptions as up-to-date as planning and writing will allow. I have rechecked with most companies at least once during the compilation of the third edition in order that the information you receive be as current as possible. At best I give you the potentialities within each company, as well as current stock and product descriptions.

What one company has perhaps discontinued is often picked up by another (the product index lists companies offering similar products), so check with a couple of them to find what you really want.

The close-outs are blessings in disguise, because things you might be yearning for (like those higher-priced covers or whatever) might be selling at 50 percent off—or better, just to clear out inventory. Sometimes a small company has got a few odd dozen of this or that diaper, or some of a certain cover they no longer carry, which you can pick up for a real bargain. So ask when you call. You never know what you'll find!

And lastly, please let the companies you buy from know you heard about them through *Diaper Changes*. This way they will know where their increased business is coming from.

Happy Perusing!

Contents

Diaper and Cover Reviews

Company Reviews

The Diaper and Cover Review Section

In the first edition of *Diaper Changes*, I had to repeat myself a lot, especially if a good product was carried by more than one company. In the interest of simplicity, I have separated out the more commonly found diaper and cover products by trade name or manufacturer, and then reviewed the products this way. This is not a replacement for reading through the company reviews, which follow this section. Some companies carry exclusive products (some rather excellent!), which are not reviewed here—and I do recommend reading the entire Resource Guide in order to get to know them. Refer back to this section when reading through the Resource Guide if necessary.

Alexis

Feather-Lite: Sometimes the more things change, the more good things remain the same. These are the pull-on diaper covers your mom or grandma may have used. They have been around forever and stand the test of time for excellent, durable fabric; simple, uncomplicated design; and low price. I love these covers and did use them very often. Made of a soft but hearty nylon, they are easy to clean and dry very quickly. Alexis used to make one of the best and least expensive snap diaper cover on the market but they have ceased production. The bindings on these are that kind of scratchy binding stuff, so if your baby has sensitive skin or you'd rather have something softer you may need to look elsewhere. Alexis also makes a vinyl version of these cover which I do not recommend.

Aristocrats

Wool soaker: This is the soaker of my dreams. The Aristocrat is an earthy, sensuous, gorgeous diaper cover—it has the heft and density of a handmade soaker and the amazing absorbability and breathability of honest, good wool. Definitely low-tech, retro, old-fashioned, and I *like* it. The wool is stretchy and not at all scratchy—a lovely tactile experience for both you and baby. It doesn't even hold the "pee-pee smell" at all! In fact you are urged to only wash this cover when soiled and air-dry at other times. Several varieties of stitching are used in the construction of this garment so you get a nice thicker section around the groin area, a wider knit at the legs (no elastic needed!), and a fold-over waistline. You can see the hand-sewn side seams. Makes you feel part of a kinder, gentler diapering universe. Aristocrats are designed to really stretch, so you only need two sizes (three to four pair per size) as opposed to four or more covers in several sizes typical of other covers of any kind. This cover will work best with a fitted diaper as the leg openings are not going to be as secure as those with elastic, so your diaper ought to have the elastic where needed to compensate.

Basic Connection

These popular covers are known for their generous size, nice fabrics, and mid-range price. They use the shorter, softer Velcro which is great to avoid rubbing, but it tends to fail my yank test. I like the paper-bag style elastic in the back—makes a good fit and a cute look.

Litewrap: This durable, well-priced Velcro cover is full cut, hardy, and easy-to-wash. A polyurethane inner coating with poly outside is preferred by diaper service customers.

Snappiwrap: For cotton and terry lovers, the Snappiwrap cover features a cotton terry outer fabric with a waterproof nylon lining. A snap at the side of each leg opening can help deter babies pulling covers off and helps prevent any Velcro rubbing.

Cottonwrap (Cot'n'wrap): This roomy cover is soft, all-cotton specially treated to be water-resistant, with short Velcro which does not abrade skin and resists lint pilling. An okay cover if you love all-cotton. Watch how you wash these, as some detergents may be too harsh. Is generally the most expensive and the least waterproof of the three Velcro covers offered.

Pull-ons: Very generously sized, very lightweight— a simple, easy-to-use cover in darker colors to help hide fecal strains. Washes well and dries super-quickly.

Doublers: These terry doublers are among the best available— thick and soft, high-quality terry. They are wider than most doublers out there and may not work for newborns or especially slim covers.

Bumkins

All-in-one: A truly hassle-free diaper and cover combination. The well-made Bumkins all-in-one is an excellent, top-of-the line product— exceedingly leakproof and works so well I can really forget to change my children at times! Bumkins have super-strong Velcro, a soft outer waterproof poly lining (which feels like nylon), and a design which lets the many layers dry relatively quickly. It fits well, washes well, endures well, and is definitely the next best thing in convenience to disposables. Bumkins is now made with a 100-percent cotton flannel quick-dry inner diaper pad.

Velcro Cover: The Bumkins nylon cover is made with a double-layer gusset, with no Lycra to get moist with the wearing. These leave no red ring, and have a mesh back panel to help keep things cool.

Bummis

This Canadian-based manufacturer has supplied some of the most popular diaper covers on the market—and with good reason. They are well-fitting, intelligently constructed, and well-priced covers using quality materials. These are great covers in the mid-price category.

Industrial Wrap (also called Super-Whisper Wrap, Super Wrap): This cover has been around a few years now—and what a Godsend! *Finally* a truly heavy-duty diaper cover that is super waterproof and that you really don't have to worry about at laundry time. I wish they had come up with this years ago! The Industrial Wrap is constructed of the heaviest polyester knit I have seen on a diaper cover—very hefty and durable. The fit is roomy so you can use it with the thicker types of diapers without worry. The Velcro folds in on itself for ease of washing—no covers sticking to your clothes or each other. You can wash these with strong detergents and not worry that they will get ruined (of course, still no bleach—but Borax, Biz, Tide, anything strong enough to really get a diaper cover clean is tolerated by these workhorse diaper covers). Please note: since this cover is so incredibly strong, dense, waterproof, and durable, those of you wanting "breathability" may want to look for lighter-weight covers or perhaps natural fiber alternatives. But look no further for heavy wetters, for trips, for overnight, or if you don't want to worry if your covers will survive the next load of laundry. I heartily recommend this hearty diaper cover!

Bummis Original: This cover features a soft, smooth, waterproof nylon with an inner mesh layer and incredibly strong Velcro. Soft Lycra bindings surround the legs and waist. These remain popular because of their lightweight softness and great fit. Worth mentioning is the particularly ingenious construction of the newborn size—the Velcro is not placed all the way up to the waist; this virtually eliminates any chance of Velcro rubbing on your newborn baby's tender new skin. You will also not have to worry about any red marks on baby's skin: the smooth, soft Lycra found on all Bummis covers does not excoriate—it's better than uncovered elastic or stitching (even if it tends to absorb more moisture). When washing, make sure the Velcro is not attached to any of the inner nylon mesh or it can snag.

Bummis Whisper Wrap: Same basic design as the original but even more lightweight and quick-drying with omission of the inner mesh layer.

Bummis pull-ons: These are a good basic pull-on made in both coated nylon and and cotton-covered styles and feature soft Lycra leg and waist bindings. Make sure you don't use anything too harsh when you wash these, and don't dry them too hot in the dryer, if at all. These are best line-dried—and they dry relatively quickly.

Cottonwood Baby Products Diapers

Formerly Blueberry Hill Babies, the diapers manufactured by Cottonwood are among the highest quality diapers available. What makes them so excellent? High quality fabrics, sensible designs, and good stitching. All Cottonwood diapers are some form of flannel/terry combo—the flannel is exceptionally soft and the terry is thicker than just about any other diapers with terry I have ever seen. You immediately feel how substantive, hefty, well-made they are—you can almost always tell a Cottonwood diaper just by the thickness of the terry alone and the well-serged pastel stitching. A beautiful combination of softness and substance.

Although some companies choose to rename these diapers, I am giving you the names as they are most commonly called.

Plushie contour: Substantive and sumptuously thick, with one layer flannel and one layer terry. While some contours only have terry in the middle, leaving the sides or periphery with just a layer or two of much thinner flannel, this has super-thick terry throughout the diaper—absorbent, long-lasting, and it does not bunch up when wet or lose its shape within the diaper cover. This is one of the diapers I grab first. Wide wings allow for pinning. In green or white cotton.

Plushie prefold: Substantial and incredibly absorbent, with the same excellent make-up as the Plushie contour. Green or white cotton and newborn, regular, and toddler sizes.

Birdseye: You might think of birdseye as flimsy, but not here! This

111

is a heavy, lovely, super-soft quality white cotton birdseye with a gorgeously thick inner terry pad. A definite favorite of mine.

Nappi: This prefold-shaped diaper is similar to the Plushie, except that is has two layers of flannel (on both sides) with an inner terry layer. Also incredibly thick, soft, and absorbent.

Diaper Service Prefolds

It's a strange world out there in diaper manufacturing land. For years Chinese diaper service diapers were considered the finest diapers available of their kind. In recent years quota restrictions have made it hard to maintain a supply equal to the demand, and thus distributors have resorted to other means of procuring necessary diapers. This goes for diaper service diapers of all kinds. Thus there is somewhat of an open arena now in the diaper service diaper universe. The main distributors are now getting diapers from other Asian countries such as Paksitan and in Europe from Estonia, although some from China are still available. Quality can really vary by batch, by country, by season. At this writing, the European diapers tend to be stronger and last longer and the Chinese tend to be softer. My best suggestion is to sample any diaper service diaper from anybody before deciding if you like them. What I tell you today may be utterly irrelevant in three months as far as the quality from a particular company is concerned.

Fuzzi Bunz

Fuzzi Bunz have joined the family of diapering products since the second edition of Diaper Changes. They are reminiscent of the old "Kangawrap" diapering system whereby a diaper is inserted between a lining and a backing (in a kind of pocket) to create a type of all-in-one. In theory, the liner draws the moisture away from baby into the diaper or padding beneath, and when you pull the diaper or padding out, it is cleaner than if the feces had been touching the diaper, making washing ultimately easier.

With Fuzzi Bunz, an insert of thick microfiber cotton terry (or you can use your own diapers) is inserted between the outer cover layer and the inner layer, which in this case is made of polyester microfleece. When soiled, you shake off the stool (or soak/rinse if you have to), separate both components and put them both into the bucket until you wash them. If, however, the diaper is only wet, you may resuse the cover (according to the company representative) by inserting another insert or diaper into the pocket.

In practice this sytem does seem to present some flaws. Indeed, their website has an entire page devoted to "troubleshooting" where you describe your problem (including leaks and feeling wet) on a feedback form.

I found these diapers to be very well made, and the design is very cute, the fit is quite good and the quality of the fabrics is excellent. I found the soil did shake easily off the very soft micro-fleece inner lining and wash up with no staining. However, the microfleece lining was still wet after I changed the inner pad. This means that when you put a fresh diaper into the Fuzzi Bunz cover/liner, old urine from the previous pee is still there. This ends up being far less clean next to the baby than one would like, plus old pee left near the skin can make diaper rash for some babies. A solution to this would be to use Fuzzi Bunz only as an all-in one, and change the cover unit every time baby pees along with the diaper/insert (you would have to get plenty of them to do this or wash frequently). This will undoubtedly be expensive for some. I am also wondering how hot polyester micro-fleece is in the hot, humid summer next to a tender baby's skin—perhaps hotter than one would like. Those of you who want only natural cotton or perhaps a bleach-free disposable diaper liner next to baby's skin will have to look elsewhere.

New trends come and go but sometimes logic and common sense are the best ways to handle old problems.

Gerber

The Gerber company has been around a long time, and over the years has changed with the times, evolving from those horrid vinyl pants (which unfortunately still exist) and thin, yucky diapers with polyester fluff (which also unfortunately still exist) to excellent Velcro covers and diaper service quality diapers. I would strongly encourage you not to buy Gerber diapers at a chain store but rather through one of the companies listed below—this way you are assured of getting the thicker, better-quality diaper service diapers rather than the inferior mass-market diapers.

Diaper Service Prefolds: These are usually offered in 6 or 8 layers. Veteran merchants inform me that the quality has varied over the years, depending on cotton crop production in the region where the diapers are being manufactured (not in the U.S. anymore—all foreign made). I would advise sampling these before investing in a large purchase—you may get an excellent batch or perhaps a batch that is thinner and not so soft.

EZ Cover: These hearty, durable, inexpensive covers remain one of my favorites. An excellent, well-built cover made with quality materials. Good strong Velcro folds in on itself for ease of washing. Made of a tough, durable poly on the inside, soft nylon on the outside, ample leg gussets and about the strongest Velcro I have seen on any diaper cover. You can give these the yank test and they come in first place. I use these a lot and they are built like more expensive covers. They wash without hassle and last forever. Please note: the poly fabric on the inside is not soft at all like many covers—it's actually a little scratchy. Best to spread the diaper well over the cover so baby feels only softness. Still, for newborns especially you may prefer a softer cover. Unbeatable for older babies. An excellent cover for the money.

Kooshies

Classic: This flannel fitted Velcro diaper features Velcro strips that are placed a little way below the top front of the diaper, to keep them from rubbing on baby's belly. It is considered by some to be an all-in-one, but because the waterproofability is not very good they are sometimes recommended to have a cover of some kind over them—which means they are really just diapers and not all-in-ones. If they are less expensive than true all-in-ones, this is why.

Ultra: This is a true all-in-one with flannel on the inside and PVC (polyvinyl chloride) for the outer layer. The smell when you open the package of diapers is really overpowering, due to the outgassing of petrochemicals used in making the vinyl. I would strongly recommend not using vinyl products near infant skin because of the potential outgassing problems and because they are incredibly unbreathable.

Nikky

Nikky brand diaper covers from Japan have been around a long time, and have proven to provide consistently high quality covers in a wide variety of styles. The fabrics and construction are superior and the covers last a very long time. The stitching is always a strong flat lock at the seams, so it feels "seamless"; the Velcro is always strong and sturdy, using little individual patches with small and tight stitching; the "fuzzy part" is softer and more like fabric itself. (Velcro is the greatest stress point on a Velcro cover, so a strong, secure Velcro piece is a necessity rather than a fancy feature for any cover.)

Nikkys are a little pricey but the quality is superb, especially for the poly styles. The designs work well with babies' physiques and the newborn styles are well-fitting, featuring an umbilical cord "dip" to help keep fabric off the cord site while healing.

One point to keep in mind is that Nikky covers are cut somewhat slim and you may need to size up if you are using especially thick diapers. Even then you will probably have to tuck the diaper into the cover some, and even then, the entire diaper may not be covered. This goes for many contour diapers as well. I would advise sampling one cover with the diaper of your choice to see if the combination you desire will work with each other and with your baby.

Wool Velcro: These water-repellent covers are the best for babies with sensitive skin and are the least likely to cause diaper rash. They last a long time and are worth the money.

All-Cotton Velcro: A super-soft fabric for cotton lovers, and makes a more realistic "water-repellent," rather than "waterproof" claim.

Breathable poly: Breathable poly is a durable double-layered poly knit with the same treatment as the all-cotton. It feels very much like cotton but will be hardier.

Heavy-Duty poly: I have been exceedingly pleased with this cover for ease of washing and durability. You will be pleased with the heavy duty poly if you do lots of laundry (or need a cover which can withstand "industrial strength" laundry habits!) and like to wash your covers with your regular loads instead of having to use some special, gentler detergent in a separate load.

Cotton/vinyl: These have been around forever but you know I hate vinyl. Still, they are built very well and are cheaper than the other Nikkys.

Training Pants: A nice-fitting garment that looks more like underpants. Not super thick, so you will want to use these at the latter end of your training period. Does have waterproofing in middle layer but only soft cotton inside and out. The "Ladybug" style has high leg openings and a knit waist which toddlers can easily work with themselves.

Bedwetter Pants: Super-absorbent pants look more like underpants and absorb up to a cup of urine. Make sure you turn these inside out when you wash them to get them really clean, and dry thoroughly. A lifesaver for me and my older bed-wetting child. We call them "night-time underpants."

Company Reviews

Angel Fluff Diaper Company
P.O. Box 1131
Lewisburg, TN 37901
800.996.2644
fax 931.359.8420
customerservice@angelfluff.com
www.angelfluff.com

Angel Fluff handcrafts quality prefold diapers in a very soft, very well-stitched white flannel. When you see these, you really can't help thinking "fluffy!" Angel Fluff prefolds are relatively thick, yet designed to dry in one cycle. The serging around the edges is far tighter and thus much more durable than much serging I have seen. Broad spectrum custom sizing is available from infants to adults. It's like having a personal seamstress!

Co-founder Jeannie Stephenson says, *"Angel Fluff Diapers was founded from a personal search for the perfect diaper at a reasonable cost. Our products are economical and environmentally friendly. We believe our 100-percent cotton fluffy diapers to be the softest diapering product for your baby's delicate skin."*

Also offered are waterproof ditty bag, diaper clips and pins, terry wipes, diaper pail liners, diaper inserts.

Angel Fluff is also a specialist in adult and youth incontinence products.

Prefolds: flannel diapers $19.95 for 6, $36.95/dozen, $32.95/dozen for 3 or more dozen. Sample $6.95 ppd. Inserts: $9.95 for 6. Diaper pail liners: $13.95, $21.95 for 2. Wipes: $6.95/dozen. Diaper Clips: $1.95/pair. Pins: $3.95 set of 4.

Aristocrats Baby Products
Box 120
Burton, B.C. Canada V0G 1E0
250.269.7343
aristo@columbiacable.net

The Aristocrats wool soaker is the cover of my dreams (see the Diaper and Cover Review Section for a full review).

Aristocrats says, *"We've been in business ten years. Our designs have been developed with comfort and utility in mind, and needless to say, they've all been tested and approved by our own three children. We hope they help make your lives a little sweeter."*

Youth sizes available.

Aristocrats is now offering a tie-on diaper with foldable inner flannel flap which allows for adjusting inside a cotton-lycra outer shell and designed to complement the Aristocrat soaker. Untying the slip-knot tie might not be easy once the diaper is saturated.

Also offered is a wool hemet hat and wool thermal knit blanket.

Prices shown are U.S. dollars. **Aristocrats:** untreated wool soakers $20–27 each, child size $33 each. Tie-on flannel diaper $10 each.

DIAPER CHANGES

As A Little Child
10701 W. 80th Ave
Arvada, CO 80005
303.456.1880

As A Little Child sells the only Gore-Tex fiber cover on the market. (Some sell Ultrex, a Gore-Tex-like fabric, with similar properties). Gore-Tex is that neat, breathable, waterproof fabric used in athletic shoes and outerwear. For an adult, the membrane works to let perspiration out and keep rain from coming in. For a baby, it keeps the wetness in and lets the moisture vapor out. This is due to the special membrane which has pores 20,000 times smaller than a drop of water, but 700 times larger than a water vapor molecule. This essentially keeps the wetness in and body heat and moisture circulating rather than trapping it inside the diaper to raise temperature and encourage bacterial growth.

I was waiting for someone to make a Gore-Tex diaper cover! The Wabby features Velcro closures which are especially strong and durable, nice nylon/Lycra bindings, easy care, and 100-percent cotton outer fabric: happy prints like trains, planes, boats, and cars, sunshine yellow, or navy blue check. This is a quality combination of breathability, ease of use, and durability in a synthetic fiber.

Owners John and Deborah Klippert say, *"As A Little Child manufactures and sells quality products for your infant and toddler which are cost-effective and healthy for both your child and the environment. When your baby wears a Wabby Gore-Tex cover, his moist body heat escapes but wetness stays inside."*

As A Little Child also carries Wabby Diapers (a quality flannel-terry combo) and Wabby Washcloths—which all together make a very good, non-complicated diapering system.

Wabby: Gore-Tex Velcro covers $12.95 each, 3 to 6 $12.25 each, 7 to 11 $11.55 each, 12 or more $10.95 each. Diapers $27.95/dozen, $25.95/dozen for 3 or more dozen. Sample diaper $2.50.

Baby Bunz and Co.

P.O. Box 113
Lynden, WA 98264
800.676.4559
fax 360.354.1203
info@babybunz.com
www.babybunz.com

This is certainly one of the most, if not the most beautiful-looking and artistically designed of the catalogs out there. Lovely, soft photos on quality paper with a pastel, baby powder touch to the whole thing. Makes you feel nice about being a Mama. An esteem-building experience when certain parts of pregnancy and postpartum make you feel less than lovely!

Baby Bunz carries an extensive line of the popular Nikky brand diaper covers. Offered are the all-cotton waterproof, breathable poly, heavy-duty poly, cotton with inner waterproof lining, and wool velcro styles. Also offered is the beautiful Aristocrats wool soaker, both the original Bummi wrap with inner mesh lining as well as the Super Industrial Wrap, the Bumkins all-in-one and two kinds of nylon pull-ons—the Bummis nylon/Lycra and another lower-priced pull-on.

Baby Bunz offers beautiful quality diapers. Each is constructed from a dense, soft flannel and very thick terry—all well designed and substantive in feel. The Cottonclouds is a lovely flannel/terry combo which can be used like a flat diaper. The Babybirdseye is constructed of high-quality birdseye fabric and a super-thick inner terry pad. The Heavenly Bottoms are a pinnable flannel/terry contour with the flannel extended all the way throughout the diaper, as well as an additional inner terry layer for better absorption and distribution and fit. Spoil Me! Snugglebottoms are a well fitting, absorbent fitted diaper with a good elastic at the legs (no elastic at the top), available with or without Velcro. These would work well with newborn babies or children with runny poop because of the snug fit where you need it! Quality diaper service prefolds are also available.

Mompreneur Carynia Van Buren (who is also the talented artist responsible for the beautiful watercolor drawing on the cover of the catalog) says: *"After over twenty years, Baby Bunz and Co. still remains committed to being a small and personal company—*

ready to help with your diapering questions. We look for well-made, durable classics—environmentally sensible, practical, and pleasing to the senses. The products we choose must be truly useful. We offer items of exceptional quality at reasonable prices and focus on offering products which make diapering easier and more enjoyable. We invite you to call us if we can be of help in any way. It's always our pleasure to serve you."

Accessories include the Diaper Duck, diaper doublers made of the same quality flannel as the diapers, flannel wipes, Weleda baby cream with calendula and zinc oxide, diaper pins, duffy sacks, a very soft, biodegradable diaper liner and pail, pottys, and toilet training aids. Swim diapers and training pants are also available as well as wool puddle pads and special no-rinse wool wash.

Other interesting offerings include wooden baby rattles, baby sheepskin moccasins, a complete set of organic cotton layettewear—including luxurious baby blankets in interlock, knit and woven fabrics, beautiful Swedish layettewear, cotton/terry dolls, a generous selection of Weleda baby products, wooden baby brushes with boar bristles, wool baby blankets, pretty children's books, and natural feeding basics for babies and children.

Baby Bunz offers a free gift surprise with any purchase over 75 dollars (excluding diapers and Nikky covers) in addition to individual diaper samples and gift certificates.

Nikky: All-cotton waterproof: $14.00–16.25 each, $13.75–15.95 each for 4 or more (sizes newborn to 3–4 year). Breathable poly: $12.50–13.95 each, $12.00–13.50 each for 4 or more (newborn to 3 year). Heavy-duty poly: $13.50–14.00 each. Cotton with waterproof liner: $11.85–13.85 each, $11.00–13.50 each for 4 or more (newborn to 3 year). Wool felt: $16.50–18.95 each, $16.00–18.50 each for 4 or more. **Prefolds:** Cottonclouds: $14.50–20.50 for 6. Babybirdseye $16.00-23.00 for 6. **Contour:** Heavenly Bottoms $18.50–24.00 for 6. Spoil Me! Snugglebottoms without Velcro $17–27 for 6, with Velcro $20–32 for 6. **Aristocrat:** wool soaker small $21, large $25 each. **Bummis:** Velcro cover $7.95 each, $7.50 each for 4 or more. Industrial Whisper Wrap $8.95–9.95 each, $8.50–9.50 each for 4 or more. Nylon pull-ons: $5.50 each, $5 each for 4 or more. **Other pull-ons:** Cheaper nylon pull-ons: $3.50 each, $3 each for 4 or more. Samples of all diapers available.

Baby Love Products/Kidalog

5015 46 St.
Camrose, Alberta T4V 3G3
780.672.1763
fax 403.672.6942
kidalog@kidalog.com
www.kidalog.com

This catalog has to be seen to be believed. Can you imagine a complete baby department store in a book? That's kind of what the Baby Love/Kidalog catalog is—all 116 full-color pages! I am not kidding you! It's so big it has its own table of contents! (And the website is equally huge! It is also easy to navigate, with all diapers and covers on one screen so it's easy to see everything of one category at once).

Sections include sleeptime (4 pages); toys, like rubberwood puzzles (34 pages); room decorations (8 pages); children's books (4 pages); parenting books (11 pages); music (12 pages); mealtime (4 pages); pregnancy and nursing (4 pages); sewing (4 pages); diapers (4 pages); potty training (2 pages); bath, grooming, and health (3 pages); and laundry, safety, footwear, going out, and twins! What else could you possibly need?

What I also like about this "book" is that all kinds of interesting (and sometimes controversial) educational material is interspersed throughout the ad copy—what amount to mini-articles on things like crib, stroller, and home safety, vaccinations, herbs not recommended during pregnancy, stroller buyer's checklist, the diaper debate, formaldehyde-treated cottons, SIDS info, buying baby clothes, and much, much more.

Diapers offered include the well-fitting Baby Softwear fitted Velcro diaper, which was designed specifically to fit perfectly inside of the Nikky brand diaper covers—and it really does. (Nikkys tend to fit kind of slim and snug, so this combination of diaper and cover works really well.) The diaper is one-size, fitting 8½ to 35 pounds, and a preemie size is offered. Extenders are available for older children's nighttime needs. The Baby Softwear diaper was given the rating of "best buy" in the Canadian Consumer Magazine's evaluation of cloth diapers and is available in organic cotton. Other fitted diapers include the Baby Love one-size diaper (also available in organic cotton), with inner panels which fold out for quicker drying, the Baby Love diaper with a polypropylene "dry skin" liner, and a waterproof version of the Baby Love diaper. The reusable polypropylene liners may also be purchased separately. Remember that the synthetic fiber will be touching baby's skin. This is a choice between softness and convenience that you will have to make. Flushable liners are also offered (which may clog some rural septic systems).

Contour diapers include Baby Love "prefolds" (these aren't square prefolds but what Americans call "contours," so don't get confused), which are also designed to fit inside the popular Nikky diaper cover, in regular and heavy-duty absorbencies, and in organic cotton. Also offered are your old-style flat square diapers and prefolds, both of flannelette.

Baby Love carries the complete line of Nikky covers (the only catalog to do so). These include the poly styles (terry velour, baby print, breathable, and heavy duty), and the all-cotton and wool styles. Other alternatives include the pull-on Feather-Lite nylon pants and the Longlife nylon pant in both pull-on and snap-on styles (an excellent replacement for the Alexis snap covers which are no longer produced). A throway version of a diaper cover is available called Babysnibbs—made of vinyl and you tie it on—but if you were to cut a garbage bag in the shape of a cover it would be about the same thing. Still, in an emergency these might be nice, as well as for camping or other travel situations where you would need to travel as light as possible. If you are looking for a lower-priced alternative to Nikkys you can find them here in the form of Spinkles Velcro covers in breathable poly, wool, and all-cotton styles.

Mompreneur Grace Marcinkowski says, *"From the perspective as a mother of four children, I have personally selected the items in the catalogue. We want to provide practical items that help you save time, and create a fun, safe, and healthy home for your little ones. I hope the items in this catalogue make parenting easier and more enjoyable. When you call during business hours, you will get a real live person, not a machine!"*

Other diaper-related products include pins, flushable and reusable diaper liners (both cloth and synthetic), locking diaper pail, the DeoDisk pail deodorizer, reusable diaper bucket liners (large and small size), ditty bags, stretch terry changing table cover, diaper bags, portable foam changing pad, wipe warmer, Nikky brand training pants, folding portable children's potty seat (the design could be better on this because it doesn't fully cover the seat!), waterproof nylon flat sheet, bed pads, the practical inflate-a-potty (great for traveling), a Swedish "heart-shaped" potty, several toilet training books, and the highly absorbent Nikky "dry bed" pants for older children. If you use wool covers or soakers, a special, lanolin-enriched cleanser helps keep them waterproof.

Baby Love offers an amazing sewing section of patterns for nursing clothing, children's wear, toys and decorations (even how to build an Indian teepee), and the Baby Softwear fitted diaper (which are a real bargain to make yourself). Special elastic, Velcro, waterproof nylon, and organic cotton are offered to make your diaper-making easy, as well as special sewing kits in regular and organic flannel which will give you 36 diapers, precut, with elastic, Velcro, sample diaper, and instructions, for a great price! All you need to do is sew!

Youth and adult diaper covers available.

I couldn't begin to tell you about other products offered by this enormous catalog. If you're looking for something, order this catalog—it's probably in here. And remember that Americans benefit from the exchange rate on the Canadian dollar, which is calculated automatically by your credit card company or bank. So figure your prices at about 30 percent lower than the prices listed in the catalog (the website shows both Canadian and U.S. prices).

Prices shown are U.S. dollars. **Baby Softwear:** fitted diaper white or print, $6.25; organic cotton, $8.95; preemie size, $7.95. With dry-skin synthetic liner, $8.95. With nylon waterproof outer layer, $8.95. Extra absorbency pads, $1.80; organic pads, $2.25. **Baby Love:** fitted diaper, $4.75; organic cotton, $7.75. With built-in waterproof pant, $8.75. With dry-skin liner, $5.95. Waterproof, with dry skin liner, $6.95. "Prefolded" (contour) $11.89–16.95 for 6; organic, $19.50–32.95 for 6. Superabsorbent (8 layer flannel), $14.70–17.70 for 6; organic, $25.20–41.58 for 6. Square flat flannel, $1.33 each. Flannel prefolds, $1.65 each. **Nikky:** terry velour, baby print, breathable poly, heavy duty poly, $19.99. All-cotton breathable, $26.60. 100-percent wool, $29.99. Training pants, $19.95. **Alexis:** Feather-lite pull-ons, $8.75 for 2. Snap-ons, $11.55 for 2. Longlife pants, $3.49.

DIAPER CHANGES

Babyworks

11725 NW West Road
Portland, OR 97229
800.422.2910
fax 503.645.4913
Bbworks@aol.com
www.babyworks.com

This catalog is pleasing to the eyes and to the touch, using the beautiful Genesis birch 100-percent recycled paper with bits and flecks of fiber, soy inks, pleasant product drawings, and interesting environmental/diapering information. Their website is easy to navigate and loads quickly. I get a nice feeling about this company every time I get their catalog.

Babyworks features the wonderful line of the popular Nikky brand of diaper covers from Japan. Another Japanese cover called Niji is offered, which is very much like the all-cotton Nikky (legs are cut a little lower for thinner babies) but for a little cheaper price. The Aristocrats pull-on wool soakers are also offered, as well as the well-priced and durable Alexis pants in pull-on style. The Litewrap from Basic Connection is also offered.

Diapers include Chinese diaper service prefolds (we are assured here that these diapers are made in a modern factory, free from human rights abuses) and a variety of the excellent diapers from Cottonwood Baby Products—the Ultimate Birdseye with thick inner terry pad, the Plushie prefold (flannel and hefty terry), the super-thick Plushie contour, and flannel prefolds (with inner thick terry pad). Also offered is green cotton contour in two sizes (designed by the owner), made to fit inside the slimmer-fitting Nikky covers. She recommends doubling these or using a doubler for overnight or extended periods as they are not as thick (especially around the periphery) as other diapers offered. Babyworks also offers the excellent Bumkins all-in-one.

Mompreneur Paula Devore says, *"Babyworks has been in business 12 years. We carry the best products we can find, in all price ranges, for many styles of diapering. All items we carry have been thoroughly tested and found to be satisfactory. In addition, we carry many other useful, natural baby products that we consider great values in their practicality, durability, and appeal. We oper-*

ate our business in a way that supports our environmental philosophy. Our catalogs are printed on 100% postconsumer recycled paper with soy ink. We strive to offer friendly, personal service and prompt shipping of your order. I feel a deep sense of gratitude that our home-based business is thriving. From our family to yours!"

Accessories include the Eucalan no-rinse wool wash, Bac-Out Stain and Odor Eliminator, a large selection of Bio-Kleen natural laundry aids, diaper pins, the Diaper Duck, duffy sacks, doublers, wipes, non-petroleum baby cream, natural baby powder (with arrowroot and clay), the Eagle Creek Parent Survival pack made of hefty Cordura Plus nylon (and an interesting design), swim diaper, 100-percent wool puddle pads, and the very good Nikky overnight pants.

Also offered are the Happy Baby food grinder (the same one I have used for 6 babies); nylon bibs; the Aubrey Organics line of bath soap, shampoo, sunblock and body lotion; natural fiber brush and comb; shea butter (a West African ointment made from pods of the shea tree); wool and cotton receiving blankets; wool baby caps; organic cotton bedding; baby layettewear and raingear; and organically grown cotton dolls (in the Waldorf tradition).

Babyworks offers a 4 or more discount and price matching on any combination of Nikky or Niji covers and discounts on Aristocrats with purchase of 3 or more. Samples are offered on all diapers with inexpensive shipping.

Nikky: All-cotton $14–16.50 each, $13.50–16 each for 4 or more. Wool Velcro $16.50–19 each, $16–18.50 each for 4 or more. Breathable and heavy-duty poly, $12.50–14.25 each, $12–13.75 each for 4 or more. Night pants $21–24 sizes 2 to 9. **Niji:** all-cotton cover $11.50–12.50 each; $11–12 each for 4 or more. **Basic Connection:** Litewrap $6.25 each; $6.00 each for 4 or more. **Aristocrats:** wool soaker $21–25 each, $20–24 each for 3 or more. **Alexis:** Feather-Lite pull-ons 2 for $6.50. **Prefolds:** diaper service $21–27 dozen. **Cottonwood Baby Products:** birdseye prefold $22–27 for 6, $42–49 per dozen. Plushie prefold $17–25 for 6, $32–47 per dozen. Unbleached Plushies $26.50 for 6; $50 per dozen. Unbleached flannel prefold $19–26 for 6, $36–49 per dozen. Toddler $32 for 6, $59 per dozen. Unbleached flannel contour $18–22 for 6, $34–40 per dozen. **Bumkins:** all-in-one $12.50 each, $11.50 each for 12 or more; $12 each for 6 or more.

DIAPER CHANGES

Barefoot Baby

P.O. Box 305
Lewis Center, OH 43035
800.735.2082
cservice@barefootbaby.com
www.barefootbaby.com

Formerly the Simple Alternatives company, Barefoot Baby continues to offer several quality diapering systems based on different situations or phases of diapering.

Barefoot Baby offers the well-made Snuggleups fitted diapers especially for newborns. They are snug around the legs (where the runny poop of a breast-fed newborn tends to get leaky) and come with or without Velcro and in white or green cotton. The Barefoot Baby diaper is also offered—a really beautiful flannel/terry combo without a thick inner pad for quicker drying, better absorbency, and better fit inside the diaper. Good, strong, soft terry, well-stitched, of good size, and available in green or white cotton.

A large variety of diaper covers and all-in-ones are offered here. Barefoot Baby sells the Bumkins and Kushies all-in-ones, as well as the newfangled Fuzzi Bunz diaper system. Bumkins also manufactures a vented diaper cover for use with regular diapers. The overlapping mesh vent in the back helps keep things cooler inside. They dry in minutes after washing and have no absorbent bindings to get wet (which does happen more often with Lycra bindings). Barefoot Baby also carries the full line of Bummis covers—their pull-on whisper pant, the Super Snap wrap, and the Super Whisper wrap—as well as the Cot'n'wrap by Basic Connection, and the beautiful Aristocrats wool soaker, and one of the thickest green cotton flannel/terry doublers I have ever seen. Barefoot Baby also sells a unique hand-made wool velcro diaper cover.

Barefoot Baby says, *"Our company was started over ten years ago to promote cloth diapering and the newer products that make cloth diapering pinless and pleasant. As we have grown over the years, these products have stood the test of time. We remain committed to customer service excellence, top-quality products, and reasonable prices. We work hard to meet your high standards. Meeting your needs is our number one priority!"*

Also offered are super-thick green cotton flannel/terry washcloths, baby wipes, swim diapers, training pants, quick-change sheet saver (bed pad), a quick-trip diaper bag, a diaper backpack, a 100-denier weight Cordura nylon diaper bag in nice colors, and the Bjorn baby carrier. Other offerings include contoured nursing pads, swimwear, and Bumkins waterproof bibs.

Washing/diapering guide included with each purchase and free shipping on all orders over $300. Gift certificates and gift registry available. Complete sample set available (one of every diaper and cover offered).

Snuggleups: White fitted diapers $31–33 for 6 with Velcro, $27 for 6 without. Green cotton $33 for 6 with Velcro, $29–30 for 6 without. **Barefoot Baby:** White diapers $16 for 6, green $21.50 for 6. **Bumkins:** All-in-one $12.95–13.95 each. Velcro cover $10–11 each. **Kooshies:** Classic $9.00 each. Ultra $9.50 each. **Fuzzi Bunz:** Cover/liner with insert $16.95, without insert $13.95 each. Basic Connection Cot'n'wrap $11 each. **Aristocrats:** Wool soaker $26.50 each. **Bummis:** Super Snap Wrap $10 each. Whisper Wrap pull-ons $6 each. Super Wrap $9.50–11 each. Individual samples of all diapers available.

DIAPER CHANGES

B. Coole Designs
2631 Piner Road
Santa Rosa, CA 95401
800.992.8924
bc@bcoole.com
www.bcoole.com

This is kind of a weird place to find cloth diapers, but they are indeed here! I really like the down-to earth feel about the work of Barbara Coole. Ms. Coole's main business is selling various kinds of distinctive clothing—dance clothes, clothing for the chemically sensitive, period clothing, untreated cottons, big sizes, plain and simple clothing. Clothing and accoutrements are dyed to order using low-impact dyes.

Ms. Coole obtains very fine quality diaper service prefolds—their size is generous, they feel especially soft and hefty before washing, and they wash and plump up beautifully. The excellent diapers are available in preemie, regular (more like a toddler size), and adult sizes. Ms. Coole also hand-sews her own flat diapers, "granny rags"/diaper doublers, and adult diapers. She will even dye your diapers in any of her light colors (lilac, sky blue, aqua, lemon, rose, apricot, bubble gum, or tan) if you like. They can even be custom-sized if you like.

Also offered are infant layette wear (dyeable in 22 color choices), nursing pads, cotton menstrual cloths, imaginative and creative art supplies and projects for children, and fabrics by the yard, including diaper fabric.

Diaper service prefolds $32 per dozen. Newborn $25 per dozen. Dyeing $4 extra per dozen.

Born to Love

445 Centre St South
Oshawa, ON L1H4C1 Canada
905.725.2559
fax 905.725.3297
catherine@borntolove.com
www.borntolove.com

This Canadian company grew up with the cloth diapering movement, having offered cotton diapering products to parents for over twenty years. This catalog had a very down-to-earth, mom-sy appeal and it is loaded with advice, tips, and encouragement. The Born to Love website is now the self-proclaimed "diapering mecca"—a large and comprehensive website offering loads of diapering, pregnancy, and parenting info, company and diaper product review sections (where you yourself can comment on a company or product) and more. Virtually all the products Born to Love sells are Canadian-made, many by moms at home. Included on the site is a currency converter for every type of currency in use—something useful for foreign customers.

Born to Love's motto is "All your baby needs, naturally!" and owner Catherine McDiarmid says, *"We celebrate over twenty years as your reliable home shopping source. At Born to Love, we are strong advocates of the personal, social, and environmental benefits of natural parenting. Our products reflect real-life needs of today's parent—like yourself, who is striving to choose just the right products for your children. Our knowledgeable customer representatives care abut your order."*

Born to Love offers several of the more popular diapers as well as many unique to Canada. Among them are Chinese diaper service prefolds (4 × 6 × 4), the Bumkins all-in-one, the Fuzzi Bunz insert combo, the Kanga-Dipe (like a Fuzzi Bunz but with cotton instead of micro-fleece lining), the Super Soaker flannel/terry combo, Hempers cotton/hemp blend prefolds (scratchy at first), and several contour and fitted diaper styles, including Cotton Kisses by Luke's Drawers, and MeeMee one-size fitted flannel diapers. The prices on many of the diapers are rather steep—some are as high as $16 per diaper (and some of these are not even all-in-ones!). Many of their diapers are in the $7–8 range, some in the $4–5 range, and only the prefolds are under $2 each (all U.S. dollars).

Born to Love offers numerous pull-on styles of covers—the

129

DIAPER CHANGES

Aristocrats wool soaker, the Bummis Whisper Pull-on in nylon and cotton styles, the Basic Connection pull-on, the Baby Kins pull on in both nylon and vinyl, the Woolums wool soaker, which can be machine-dried, and a side-snap cover that does a very good job of replacing the old Alexis snap covers. Other covers include the complete line of Bummis Velcro covers, the complete line of Basic Connection, a cute hand-knitted and chrocheted velcro wool cover, and two snap wool style soakers by Woolums. Other styles of diapers and covers are offered.

Born to Love also offers disposable diaper liners, duffy sacks, the Diaper Duck, waterproof crib pads, travel potty seat, and training pants.

Other interesting items include 6 different diaper/cover patterns, the wonderful Elizabeth Lee Designs nursing clothes patterns, nursing bras, breast pump, reusable menstrual products, a large selection of Weleda and Simply Divine baby care products, unpetroleum jelly, Dr. Bronner's Soap (yeah!), the Nature Clean line of citrus, corn, and coconut cleaning products including organic laundry powder and laundry stain remover, baby slings, safety devices, bibs, infant clothes, and books. Born to Love has also recently opened an online toy store!

An incredibly complete fitting guide is available which gives waist, depth, crotch, and leg measurements for every diaper and cover offered by Born to Love! Absorbency measurements and drying times are also given (a very scientific and intellectual way of dealing with diapers!). Also available is a brochure on how to choose the perfect diaper—which might help you since Born to Love offers so many products! Diaper/cover sample packs offered as well as a good selection of incontinence products for older children.

Prices are shown in U.S. dollars. *Diaper prices are per piece, not per dozen,* and decrease as you order by the dozen or dozens. **Chinese diaper service prefolds:** $1.94. **Super Soaker** flannel terry combo $4.54–5.52. **Hempers** hemp/cotton prefolds $9.39. **Cotton Kisses** fitted diapers 16.22. **MeeMee** fitted diaper $11.02. **Fuzzi Bunz** $14.27 no insert, $16.22 w/insert, extra inserts $5.71. **Bumkins** $14.27. **Babykins** Vinyl $1.92, Nylon $3.57. **Bummis** nylon pull-on $7.49. Nylon Velcro $8. Industrial Wrap $8.65. Industrial snap $9.75. Cotton Covers $10.85. **Basic Connection** pull-on $5.52. **AJ's Wool Soaker** $14.94. **Woolums** soaker $24.67. **Aristocrats** wool soaker $19.47. **Snap to fit:** woolwrap, woven or knitted $26.62. Side snap $6.47.

Diaperaps
19635 Business Center Dr. #7
Northridge, CA 91324
800.477.3424
fax 818.886.4033
service@diaperaps.com
www.ebabydiaper.com / www.diaperaps.com

Diaperaps was one of the first companies to come up with modern, pinless diapering. President and inventor Rachel Flug, mother of three, says, "*I developed my products out of my personal commitment to creating healthy, comfortable, and environmentally friendly products for babies. We have been the leader and innovator in this category for sixteen years. We have received numerous awards recognizing our environmental commitment as well as our manufacturing talents. I have worked for many years perfecting these products. I hope my work will make your decisions easier.*"

Diaperaps diaper covers feature a waterproof polyurethane bonded to either a durable cotton/poly knit or 100% polyester in both solids and prints. (I really love the lightweight, soft, and durable poly fabric.) The Velcro covers feature especially large side gussets—a feature I really like.) Their pull-ons are inexpensive, durable, long-wearing, hardy, easy to clean (the stool just slides off the slick urethane coating), and are stain resistant. An extra "finger tab" is offered on the cotton style which helps keep baby from pulling cover off (but a determined toddler or baby will figure it out anyway, experience shows me).

Diaperaps also offers diaper service prefolds in small and regular sizes and in six and eight layers. Prefolds with poly inner pad are offered, as well as a four-layer diaper but I don't recommend these. Thick gauze doublers are also offered.

Training pants are available in cotton knit with a hidden waterproof layer as well as swim diapers and diaper swim suits; 100-percent biodegradable liners and big diaper totes are also offered.

Quantity discounts on both diapers and covers and diaper samples available. **Diaperaps:** Cotton blend knit $8.50–9.50 each. Poly knit $8–9 each. Diaper protector cover $9.50–10.50 each. Pull ons newborn and small only $4 each. **Diaper service prefolds:** 4 × 8 × 4 $29 per dozen; 4 × 6 × 4 regular $24 per dozen; 4 × 6 × 4 small $19 per dozen.

DIAPER CHANGES

Ecobaby Organics
332 Coogan Way
El Cajon, CA 92020
888.ECOBABY
619.562.9606
fax 619.562.0199
ginny@ecobaby.com
www.natural-baby.com
www.ecobaby.com

Ecobaby's catalog and website are bright, happy, and colorful, featuring a quantity and quality assortment of green and organic cotton diapers, bedding, clothing, and accessories. All-in-ones include the Kooshies Ultra and Classic, the excellent Bumkins, and the newfangled Fuzzi Bunz (which when assembled acts as an all-in-one). Ecobaby recommends using the Kooshies only if you plan to change them very often, as they tend to leak more quickly than the other all-in-ones offered. One may also use a pull-on pant over these—but it seems just extra work and hassle to me when the other all-in-ones work so much better—even if they are more expensive (and it kind of defeats the point of using an all-in one!).

Wool covers include four beautiful styles—the Staccinator wool snap wrap (the only snap wool cover available on the American market) in three happy colors instead of plain uncolored wool, the gorgeous and well-built Aristocrats soaker, a Velcro wool cover made in Germany (big and thick wool), and a "basic" wool cover about half the price of the Aristocrats but significantly thinner in density and not as well crafted. Other covers include the excellent Bummis Whisper Wrap as well as the cotton-covered style (which can absorb wetness on the outside of the cover), as well as Super Wrap styles in snap or Velcro, the adorable Polar Babies Polartec fleece Velcro cover, a Velcro cover made by Bumkins with an "air-flow" panel on the back side, and the Cot'n'wraps cotton and Velcro combination.

Diapers include several lovely organic styles—rectangular (in two sizes), contoured (in two sizes) a deluxe prefold (all made of extremely soft cotton sherpa), an organic fitted diaper in both velcro and an unusual tie-on style (which can be difficult to untie when wet and you have a wriggly baby), and two organic snap terry diapers which model the adjustable snap Mother-ease style for the one-size and cute "paper bag" style on the back for the "absorb-it-all" style, which is very similar to the Mother-ease Sandy's diaper. The rectangular and contoured diapers are available in unbleached non-organic styles as well, both in three sizes including child/toddler.

Other diaper-related products include dioxin-free disposable diaper liners, zeolite natural odor-eater, safe plastic polyolefin diaper pail, Eucalan wool wash, bedwetter pants, potty chairs, three kinds of training pants, swim diapers in cute designs, Bac-Out waste and odor digestor and natural laundry products. Ointments and lotions include the Aubrey Organics line and the Badger line of herbal balms.

Ecobaby has the most comprehensive and beautiful offering of organic products available anywhere. If you want something organic, you will probably find it here! Products include organic crib and adult bedding (including bed and mattress pads, chemical-free mattresses, cotton and wool blankets and comforters); wooden children's playroom and bedroom furniture; wooden toys, rattles, puzzles, games, and musical instruments; and a huge selection of organic clothing for babies, kids, and moms, including nursingwear.

Kushies: Ultra $10.99–12.29 each, $45.99–55.99 for a 5-pack. Kushies Classics $8.99–11 each, $79.99 for a 10-pack, toddler $49.95 for a 5-pack. **Bumkins:** $14.99 each, 5 for $69.99. Youth sizes available. **Staccinator:** snap wool cover $19.99 each. **Kid** wool velcro cover $24.99 each. **Aristocrats:** pull-on wool soaker $26.99–39.99 each. Basic wool diaper cover $13.99–18.99 each. **Bummis:** whisper wrap $8.60 each. Cotton covered $10.99 each. Bummis Super Snap Wrap velcro style $8.99. Snap wrap $9.99 each. Pull-ons $5.99–8.50 each. **Basic Connection:** Cot'n'wraps $11.99 each. **Polar Babies:** Polartec cover $19.50–19.99 each. **Fuzzi Bunz:** diaper covers $11.99–17.99 each. Inserts $7.50 for a 3-pack. **Diapers:** Unbleached rectangular/contours, $17.99–21.99 for a 5-pack. **Organic:** rectangular $16.99–19.99 for a 3-pack. Organic contour $15.99–17.99 for a 3-pack. Deluxe prefold $23.99 for a 3-pack. Organic snap one-size diaper $12.99 each, 5 for $54.99. Absorb-it-all organic diaper in 3 sizes, $17.99 each. Organic fitted velcro diaper $8.99–12.99 each. Tie-style organic diaper $8.99 each.

DIAPER CHANGES

Gaiam/Harmony
360 Interlocken Boulevard, Suite 300
Broomfield, CO 80021
800.869.3446
fax 800.456.1139
www.gaiam.com

This is a resource for environmentally-friendly (and environmentally-correct) products. Their clothing and bedding are gorgeous! Offered are items which use new dyeing methods without petrochemicals, such as color-grown cottons, natural, organic plant and mineral dyes, and low-impact dyes. Additionally, you will find a host of body care, home decorating, gardening, health, and cleaning products. Their website is humongous with seven catalog-representative sites within it, featuring other aspects of natural living such as solar energy, fitness, travel, whole foods and body health. (To find the cleaning agents, click on the "home and outdoor" link and then the "household tools and cleaning" link.)

For cleaning diapers, Harmony offers the 7th Generation brand of concentrated, biodegradable, fragrance- and dye-free laundry powder, citrus-scented liquid detergent, and non-chlorine bleach. Fabric softener, unbleached paper products, garbage bags, dish soap, all-purpose cleaners, alcohol-free baby wipes, wooden drying racks, and a host of other chlorine-free and low-impact products are available. Automatic delivery program available which sends regularly-needed products on schedule without any shipping charges.

Cleaning agents: Laundry powder 48 oz. (18 loads) per box, $10.95 for 2 boxes, $47.95 for 10 boxes; 112 oz. (42 loads) per box, $21.95 for 2 boxes, $38.95 for 4 boxes. Liquid laundry detergent 50 oz. (16 loads) per bottle, $10.95 for 2 bottles; 100 oz. (33 loads) per bottle, $18.50 for 2 bottles, $49.95 for 6 bottles. Non-chlorine bleach 64 oz. bottles $7.50 for 2, $19.95 for 6.

GVS Distributors

The Company and Resource Guide

P.O. Box 310
Versailles, MO 65084
800.398.2494
fax 573.378.2100

And now for something completely different! GVS caters mainly to the large Amish and Mennonite populations in the U.S. You will enter the world of a thriving subculture and see what people do without TV and other entertainment. As I've mentioned before, you'll see a lot of polyester here, and acrylic things. Ah well. At least they love cloth diapering!

GVS carries Gerber diaper service quality diapers (which I recommend) and Gerber's two other kinds (which I would not recommend). For covers, the only ones I can recommend from this catalog are the Alexis Feather-Lite pull-ons.

GVS is an incredible source of sewing supplies—after all, the Plain People make just about everything they wear! Impressive children's toys, homespun a capella hymn tapes, lots of innocent children's books, maternity belts, Usborne and Dover book titles, tons of stickers, nursing slips and bras, and pumps, among other things, complete the offering.

Please note however: a popular toy among the Plain People, which they sell in this catalog, are bead necklaces which are definitely not chokeproof. Please do not buy these as they can pull apart and be very dangerous. I have always been worried when I see babies pulling and biting on those little beads!

Prefolds: Gerber diaper service prefolds $9.89 for 6. **Alexis:** Feather-Lite nylon pull-ons $5.69 for a 2-pack. Discounts with quantity purchases.

Hip Baby
2110 West 4th Avenue
Vancouver, BC V6K IN6
888.HIPBABY
info@hipbaby.com
www.hipbaby.com

Hip Baby has brought urban parenting to the Internet. The Hip Baby website says, *"Hip Baby provides useful equipment for intelligent parenting. Our emphasis is environmentally friendly products to delight discerning mothers, curious infants and appreciative fathers. Many of our products are made exclusively for us and aren't available anywhere else. Everything is tested by us and our children, and is the result of careful selection and design. We are always available to answer your questions and explain our products. Most of our friendly staff are parents like you, who can talk from experience."* Their website provides "hiptips" for issues like introducing solid foods, breast engorgement, and travelling with children.

Hip Baby carries its own Snug to Fit diaper, constructed of 100-percent flannel and Velcro in white or natural; a shaped flannel flat diaper (requires pins); the Basic Connection Pro-Rap Velcro cover; and the Aristocrats wool soaker. Also offered are a lovely array of balms and ointments containing things like camomile, calendula, anti-fungal herbs, as well as alcohol-free Tushies Wipes.

Hip Baby also carries bath time aids, baby sling, diaper bag suitcase, utensils, bottle-related products, breast pumps and paraphernalia, and many interesting toys and children's books.

Hipbaby: Snug to Fit Diaper $12 each, buy 12 get one free. Shaped flannel flat diaper $35 per dozen. **Basic Connection:** Pro-Rap cover: $12.95 each. **Aristocrats:** wool soaker $34.

Homeschool World
P.O. Box 1250
Fenton, MO 63026
800.3HOME22
fax 314.343.7423
svc@home-school.com
www.home-school.com

This is primarily a company servicing Christian homeschoolers and offers books, educational materials, and other related items as well as a quarterly magazine. Their website has developed into a tremedously detailed hub for homeschooling news and networking. Homeschool World does, however, sell the diaper service twill diapers from Gerber in size small and large. Sample pack offered.

Gerber: diaper service diapers $20 newborns, $25 regular size. Sample pack $5.

Land's End
1 Land's End Lane
Dodgeville, WI 53595
800.963.4816
fax 800.332.0103
www.landsend.com

Many of you will be familiar with Land's End as one of the largest mail order purveyors of quality merchandise, ranging from fine clothing to bedding to sports gear and much more. It also happens to be the place to get good quality diaper bags.

The Do-It-All Diaper Bag is their base model diaper bag, made with 400 Denier nylon (lined with vinyl). It has a matching nylon changing pad, several compartments, bottle pockets, and a removable waterproof pouch. Their deluxe model has an expandable hanging toiletry kit and extra-large water-resistant pouch. Instead of chintzy, tacky designs, these are made in solid colors—black, deep forest, navy, pumpkin, bright red, dusty turqoise, raisin—all of which are stylish enough for a father to sling over his shoulder or for anyone to take on non-diapering excursions. Two other designs offered are the backpack diaper bag, made of tough 600-denier polyester, with detachable zippered bag for wet items, insulated bottle pockets, a see-through plastic pouch to hold all those little things you need to carry, and waterproof changing pad. The design on this looks like a regular, high-quality diaper bag. The Little Tripper is a tote that, for under 20 bucks, even has a changing pad and 400 denier nylon and even a water-resistant pouch and toiletry kit!

Land's End carries a separate kids' catalog with clothing and accessories from birth to teens as well as high quality bedding and business clothing and much more.

Diaper bags: Do-It-All diaper bag solid colors $29.50. Deluxe Diaper Bag $49.50. Backpack diaper bag $39.50. Little Tripper $19.50.

DIAPER CHANGES

Lill-ing
P.O. Box 3571
Vero Beach, FL 32964
800.747.WOOL
fax 561.234.6963
www.lill-ing.net

Oh, I really love these darling wool soakers! The Lill-ing Company imports high quality, untreated and undyed Ruskovilla merino wool from Finland. The resulting soakers are a finely knitted, incredibly soft and touchable fabric which is truly a garment, not just a diaper cover. (Wool is a gorgeous fabric for babies, especially newborn babies. It is naturally water-repellent, absorbs 30 to 40 percent of its own weight in moisture without feeling wet, is highly breathable, insulating, naturally flame-resistant, keeps cool in summer and warm in winter, resists bacterial growth . . . need I say more?)

Lill-ing says, *"Our wool products are made from 100 percent natural Merino wool, without any chemical tratment whatsoever. Just pure softness to cradle your little ones and bring warmth to your entire family."*

The "nappy pants" offered are really more like clothing than soakers—in fact, one could easily use the long-legged version as a combination soaker/legging and the short version as a soaker/bloomer. The waist is made extra long, so it folds down to fit (no elastic anywhere!). These are truly gorgeous, wonderful to the touch, adorable-looking, and functional.

Lill-ing even sells a flat square diaper in "soda-washed cotton" which must be folded but is fast-drying.

Also offered in varieties of wool knit, silk, wool/silk combinations, and wool tricot are baby shirts, silk baby bonnets, rompers, swaddling cloths, buntings, sleeping sacks, blankets, socks, mittens, hats, long johns, and onesies. Preemie sizes available. Wool and wool blend leggings, long johns, shirts, socks, and hats for adults available also. This stuff is absolutely gorgeous!

Wool Soakers: Short leg nappy pants $21 each. Long leg nappy pants $23.50–25.50 each. **Other products:** Eucalan wool wash 16.9 oz. for $9.99. Lavender Eucalan (ah!) 8.4 oz. for $4.99. Flat square diaper sample $3.50.

Mia Bambini
360 Merrimack Street
Lawrence, MA 01843
978.682.3600
mia@miabambini.com
www.miabambini.com

Mia Bambini is now the exclusive manufacturer and retailer of the wonderful Biobottoms line of diaper covers (the baby on the cover of this book, my fourth child, is wearing a Biobottoms cover!). These are one of my all-time favorites. They are made exquisitely well and last a long time. Besides the quality, the design is very cute—the elastic of the cover gathers in the back in a "paper bag" style—looks very appealing on babies. The Velcro is very strong and the fuzzy part where the hook part catches is softer than others out there. I really consider Biobottoms work of art, a masterpiece of construction!

Biobottoms come in three styles of wool diaper covers. The Classic is full-cut for maximum coverage. The Rainbow is the same cut but with bright rainbow stitching around the edges. The Rainbow Bikini has a wide leg cut for a very good fit with either very chubby legs or very thin legs. The Cottonbottoms cotton covers are lined with waterproof, poly knit and come in four outer terry colors choices. These are extremely durable and you can't ruin these. Snaps are included in larger sizes to help deter babies pulling them off.

Stay-dry pull-on pants are also offered which can absorb up to a cup of urine. Also featured is a cute line of baby and children's clothes including swimwear, footwear, and accessories.

Biobottoms: Classic and Rainbow and Bikini 20.00 each. Full and Bikini-Cut Cottonbottoms 18.00 each Stay-dry pants 28.00. Swim diaper 9.50.

DIAPER CHANGES

Mother-ease

6391 Walmore Road
Niagara Falls, NY 14034
800.416.1475
fax 905.988.1110
diapers@mother-ease.com
www.mother-ease.com

These diapers and covers deserve a lot of superlatives. Mother-ease products have received my highest praise before, and again I offer them to you as among the finest diapers and covers made today. Mother-ease fitted diapers are intelligently crafted from one of the softest diaper materials I have ever felt, an exceedingly gorgeous, luxuriously soft, brushed cotton terry knit which is like nothing else. This is definitely not the heavy, often coarse terry you're thinking about. You immediately see the quality materials and workmanship put into these little "works of art," as I like to call them. These diapers would be perfect for newborns when you might want the softest cotton available next to your new baby's skin. (Yes, yes, I know there's 14 percent poly in the terry used—but believe me, you never feel it, it keeps the diapers very strong, and this is the one time where it really seems to make a better diaper.) Plus, if you are a Velcro hater, you have come to the right place—both diaper styles, one cover style, and their all-in-ones have sturdy plastic snaps—an improvement over old-fashioned metal snaps which can get too cold or too hot. All Mother-ease diapers would work well for heavy wetters, as they rank among the most absorbent diapers available. Both styles are elasticized, fit well, and come in white and unbleached material. Really very different and very lovely, especially in green cotton.

Because they are so hefty and substantial, Mother-ease diapers will take longer to dry than the average conventional diapers, though the one-size somewhat less than the Sandy's and the all-in-one the longest of the three.

It's not just the fabric used, the intelligent design, and the sheer beauty of the diapers themselves, but how easy it is to use the Mother-ease system that makes this such an excellent diapering choice. I have used Mother-ease diapers with either a pull-on cover or a snap-on cover. You get an excellent fit, the diaper never sags or falls off, it is easy to take on and off, washing is easy—(no Velcro to get stuck on each other), and hassle-free—if you like pull-ons or snap on covers you don't have to run around looking for your pins or clips or what have you. As I have been mother of six children, at times with three in diapers (two full-time and one part-timer at night) I can tell you I appreciate the ease that Mother-ease diapers brought to those busy times of my life.

The Sandy's fitted, three-size diaper is a cute, plump, paper-bag design with lots of center padding and snaps at the side rather than in the front. You feel the heft and thickness of these hearty, great-fitting diapers. Great for overnight or your heaviest wetters, and well worth the extra drying time. You have to be careful to dry the Sandy's thoroughly or they may over time begin to retain some mildewy-pee smell; I recommend soaking these in baking soda before washing and making sure they are dried thoroughly (even run through an extra drying cycle) just to be sure they are completely dry.

The Mother-ease One-Size diaper is one amazing diaper. Intelligently constructed, with snaps in strategic locations on both sides of the diaper to give a true custom fit for newborns through toddlers. Extra snap-on doublers are available, which enable the one-size to be as absorbent as the Sandy's but quicker (and more completely) drying. Both styles are elasticized, fit well, are thick and highly absorbent, and come in white and unbleached material. You feel the heft and thickness of these diapers. I envision a beautiful combination of the unbleached Sandy's with a wool soaker or wool Velcro cover.

The all-in-one uses a soft laminated poly knit outer layer, cotton terry in the middle, and flannel to touch the skin. This fits well even without Velcro because the elastic gives a snug fit and the snaps are spaced apart to allow for growth. Because the all-in-ones are so thick, they will take a long time to dry—you might need an hour and a half or more in the dryer to dry a load. The most absorbent I've seen anywhere. It is a very good product for the extra effort it might take. For super heavy wetters or long hauls overnight it would be a first choice.

The proprietor also suggests using the all-in-ones as a supplemental, rather than a primary diapering system to help them last longer and save money.

Diaper covers include the Air-flow snap cover and the Rikki wrap. The Air-flow is full cut like a pull-on but much easier to use, with adjustable snaps and industrial-strength, poly-backed urethane for hard work. This cover washes and dries beautifully, as the poop just slides off the slick coating. The leg bindings are not the soft Lycra often seen these days, but some people prefer covers without Lycra because Lycra tends to absorb moisture pretty quickly even if the cover stays dry. (Fitted diapers need to be used.) The Rikki Wrap is a Velcro cover with strong Aplix Velcro-like closures. Both are soft knit poly bonded to urethane—very, very waterproof and a good durable cover choice. These diapers wash extremely well and are very hardy. The Velcro style has an extra panel behind the stitching to keep moisture from getting through the front panel (a common problem with Velcro diaper covers). Yet another mark of genius in craftsmanship!

Both style diapers come with the newly popular 100-percent polyester "stay-dry" liners, which are supposed to keep wetness off baby. Mother-ease designs are better than some because they are designed to be single-use—not reusing a cover/liner combo with the previous change's pee still on it. Still, I wonder how much hotter poly will be in the summer next to baby's skin. The One-Size comes in both sewn-in and snap-in liner styles; the Sandy's comes in a lay-in style.

Also available are non-flushable, throwaway diaper liners, separate stay-dry liners, training pants to 60 pounds, bed-wetter pants to 65 pounds (very thick and absorbent), adjustable swim diaper with poop catcher, and nursing pads.

Special offers include buy twelve diapers get one free, moneysaving introductory sample offer, starter package, part-time package, convenience package, cover special, and complete packages which save significantly on buying items separately. Shipping is only three bucks on all orders and two bucks handling charge on all orders under 50 dollars.

Mother-ease: One-size $8.95 each. One-size dry $10.95. Snap liner $1.95 each. Snap-in dry liner $2.95 each. Sandy's $8.95–9.50 each. Toddle-ease $10.50. Sandy's liner $1.50–1.80. Dry liner $2.40 each. Air Flow, Rikki covers $9.75–10.50 each. All-in-one $13.95–14.95.

The Natural Baby Catalog/Kids Club
7090 Whipple Ave
North Canton, OH 44720-6907
888.550.2461/800.363.0500
fax 330.492.8251
www.kidsstuff.com

The Natural Baby Catalog offers diapering products as well as gorgeous children's products ranging from toys to bedding to furniture and more. I've been particularly impressed with their collection of wooden toys—definitely not hyper-tech, one-time plastic gadgets, but keepsakes of quality. The kidsstuff.com website is comprised of three companies which are now part of the same conglomerate: Kid's Club, Perfectly Safe, and Natural Baby.

Natural Baby says, *"We are committed to bringing simplicity, quality, and all natural, ecologically-minded products to you and your children. We are a safe haven where everything natural defines the contents of our catalog. Each fine-quality item is made from things of the earth—that just makes good sense to us."*

For covers, three excellent and popular Nikky Velcro covers are offered—the wool felt, treated all-cotton, and the vinyl with outer cotton layer. The Elan specially treated all-cotton Velcro cover is available with an umbilical cord dip for newborns, and is about five dollars less per cover than the comparable Nikky. These are lighter in weight, less water-resistant and stretchier than the Nikky fabric, and have what amounts to regular elastic around the legs rather than the softer, more durable poly binding found on the Nikkys. The Reuz'M all-in-one snap diaper is quick drying (with fold out inner panels) and absorbent. You may not get the firmest fit with these. The Reuz'M comes in loads of colorful, happy prints as well.

A very nice, inexpensive, knit wool soaker from Australia is available—well constructed with thicker knit at the bottom of the soaker—has the look and feel of a hand-knitted Afghan or mittens or a scarf. The fit is a little snug at the legs so if you have a chubby baby these may not work for you.

Currently offered by Natural Baby is an organic snap diaper by Under the Nile which has optional snap-in liner. (These tend to wear

143

out faster than non-organic styles, though they are very soft.) Also offered is their own birdseye contour diaper which is too thin to recommend.

Accoutrements include the same locking diaper pail that I use, washable, bleachable nylon diaper pail liners (a real lifesaver), wipe warmer, an excellent, durable nylon changing pad, wool puddle pads in sizes small through queen size, wipes, wooden potty, training pants, and calendula herbal baby oil.

Natural Baby also carries many visually appealing toys. Wooden toys include a dump truck, trains, airplanes, horse and cart, Skwishes, bead baby, play phone and camera, bead bunny, clown, bear, man, tons of rattles in happy rainbow and primary colors, carpenter tools, lawn mower, push puppets, maple ring rattle and clacker, nesting boxes, trike, jump ropes, a full usable kitchen set with washing machine, sink, ironing board, dishwasher, fridge, and pots and pans, German-made puzzles (a feast for the eyes), non-plastic busy box, walker, ring stacker, slide/play area, barn set, rocking horse, shape sorter, doll furniture. Feeding and grooming sets, handmade cotton dolls stuffed with wool, wool lambies, wool stuffed animals, and handmade doll clothing complement the wooden offerings. A complete children's bedroom of non-toxic furniture, non-chemical crib mattress, wool pillow, and green and organic cotton bedding are also offered.

A collection of organic clothing made from low-impact dyes, and a layette of silky wool underthings for baby are available.

Natural Baby also has nursing bras, clothes, and accessories; a complete line of home remedies and herbs; plenty of reading material; gorgeous German art supplies of the highest quality; wooden toothbrushes; and hard-to-find cotton and wool tights and socks!

I would also encourage you to check out the adjacent Perfectly Safe website/catalog for their offerings of safety items for every room of your home, as well as toilet training and nighttime bedding needs.

Organic: snap diapers 4 diapers for $34.95. One diaper $14.95. Natural Baby birdseye contour $20–22.95 dozen. **Nikky:** cotton cover $19.95 each. Wool $24.95 each. Cotton with waterproof layer $14.36–15.96 each. Bedwetter pants: $27.95 each **Elan:** cotton velcro cover $12.95 each. **Reuz'M:** all-in-one $14.95. **Wool soaker:** $11.96 each.

Polar Babies

P.O. Box 10953
Eugene, OR 07440
877.595.5901
fax 541.344.7878
Jessica@diapercovers.com
www.diapercovers.com
www.polarbabies.com

What a refreshingly different kind of diaper cover! How about wrapping your baby in recycled plastic soda bottles? Yes, it's here, and it's gorgeous. The Bear Bottoms cover is really a paradigm shift in the way we think about and make diapering products. What struck me when I first sampled the Bear Bottoms was the amazingly soft texture—the best of what a synthetic fabric can be. It's kind of wooly—a high quality, breathable polar fleece (not the yukky, pilly, unattractive stuff you're thinking about). Very sensuous to the touch. *Mmmmmmm.....*

Bear Bottoms has excellent Velcro which passed my ultra-tough yank test, a very cute paper bag–style waist, an inner "waterproof/ breathable" lining made of a fiber called "Windbloc" fleece, which, like Gore-Tex and Ultrex, allows water vapor to escape but not the wetness itself, and comes in either luscious deep purple (and I mean *deep*), or recycled natural (which is reminiscent of wool covers. Who says synthetics are all bad?) The quality of workmanship in these covers reminds me more of fine clothing than a diapering product.

Bear Bottoms wash up beautifully (no fecal stains left at all). Powdered rather than liquid detergent is recommended. The fit is a little snug so you will want to size up at least a size if you are using a very thick terry or other heavy diaper. Because it is essentially the synthetic cousin of wool, Bear Bottoms may work in lieu of wool for babies with wool sensitivities.

I am very impressed with Polar Babies new, amazing hemp/cotton blend prefold diaper—this thing will change your mind about hemp. This diaper feels like fine soft wool, without any itchiness. You would not know there was any hemp in it, it is so soft. Unbelievable. These are pricey but you could buy some individual diapers just for heavy-wetting nighttime needs or traveling if you prefer. Also offered is a hemp/terry doubler with polar fleece lining, as well as hemp washcloths!

Jessica says, *"I developed Polar Babies Polartec fleece diaper covers as an alternative for mothers who need the breathability of wool, yet are concerned about wool sensitivities in their babies. Fleece is much easier to care for than wool. My goal is to provide an excellent performance product that encourages parents to consider cloth diapering, not only because of its benefits to the environment and pocketbook, but because of the superior performance of today's age of high-tech fabrics."*

Polar Babies also offers clothing made from the same gorgeous polar fleece: hooded jacket, pants, bunting, booties, mitties, blankies, and hats, in such colors as midnight, royal, and marine blue; hunter green; rosewood burgundy; deep teal green; and the incredibly rich concord purple of the diaper covers.

Polar Babies: diaper covers, all sizes, $18–20 each. **Hemp:** prefolds $6.50–8.50 each, $70–90 per dozen.

Tushies
675 Industrial Blvd.
Delta. CO 81416
800.344.6379
fax 970.874.5405
tushies123@aol.com
www.tushies.com

This disposable used to call itself "the alternative diaper." I think we all know that the only truly alternative diaper these days is the cloth diaper—not a disposable of any kind. Now they have renamed the Tushies disposable as "the gel-free alternative diaper." Better, but it would be more honest yet to say "gel-free alternative disposable diaper," as all cloth diapers are gel-free and always have been. Their current motto is "change the world one diaper at a time." And how exactly do you do that by continuing to add to the tons of disposable diapers already in our nation's landfills?

Tushies does not use sodium polyacrylate in the absorbent fluff layer of the diaper. You are encouraged to cut a regular disposable up and pour the insides into a jar, then pour water on it and be grossed out as it turns to a solid gel. Rather than hyping a super-thin disposable, as is the vogue of today's standard disposable manufacturers, Tushies is happy that theirs are nice and thick, full of wood pulp and "high absorbency natural-blend cotton padding." It heralds a "cloth-like" cellulose cover (which is a matter of opinion, really) , rather than the cornstarch-based backing of previous styles. Tushies are also free of perfumes and dyes and I am happy to report that Tushies is now using "non–chlorine bleached wood pulp" in its dispoable diapers. I would not be surprised if what I said in the second edition about their previous use of elemental-chlorine-free pulp didn't change their practices through consumer education. Well, good for them, they have made a great step forward, but Tushies gel-free alternative disposable diapers are still going to wind up in landfills and creating solid waste.

Tushies uses at least 25 percent cotton in their padding layer. Remember that this is surgical grade cotton, but not organic cotton. I question the use of a reusable resource such as cotton in a throwaway product such as disposable diaper.

It is encouraging to see a disposable made without sodium polyacrylate, to show that it can be done and that parents will buy it. No baby needs any unnecessary chemicals on his tender skin, especially on his vulnerable genital tissues during his formative years. This would be the primary reason why I would recommend these disposables to any parent.

Use them (if you can afford them!), for trips or other special situations, and then write to your old disposable company and tell them why you chose a gel-free disposable—and better yet, why you use cloth diapers the better part of the time! But please remember, parents, that a disposable-with-cotton-on-the-inside-and-cotton-like-cover-on-the-outside is still a disposable, which takes up landfill space like any other, is still unreusable, and still contributes to our solid waste problem.

I must stress that the only truly "alternative" diaper is the cloth diaper, and a truly environmentally respectful disposable—whatever that may be someday—has yet to appear on the market.

Other Tushies products include Tushies alcohol-free wipes with aloe vera, Tushies Mates inserts to be used inside the disposable diaper for added absorbency, and a secure corner safety fitted crib sheet.

Diapers and other products are delivered to your door and the club prices include shipping.

Tushies: preemie/newborn case (270 diapers) $48; club price $7.99 bag of 30. Small case (160 diapers) $43.96; club price $35.96. Medium case (120 diapers) $43.96; club price $35.96. Large case (88 diapers) $43.96; club price $35.96. Toddler case (80 diapers) $43.96; club price $35.96.

DIAPER CHANGES

WeeBees Essential Baby Products
3100 S Sheridan Blvd Unit 1C PMB 200
Denver, CO 80227
877. WEE BEES
fax 888.697.BABY
info@weebees.com
www.weebees.com

An experienced family of eight (six boys!) is behind this down-to-earth diapering company. The Wiebe's approach is to help you diaper in the least expensive, most practical and hassle-free manner possible, using quality products. Having had three in diapers at a time several times, this family obviously knows their stuff for minimalist, burden-free home diapering. And they've sure got a lot more to do than change diapers all day!

WeeBees offers high-quality diaper service diapers in preemie, newborn, regular, and toddler sizes, in either 6 or 8 layer construction. She offers both the softer Chinese diapers in both white and unbleached and the stronger and more durable European diaper service diapers. Genuine Australian nappy diapers—which are like huge terry hand towels (the old-fashioned way and popular in Europe) are also available. She also carries hemp-blend prefold diapers. Rhonda also recently introduced her own WeeBees Adjustable Snap-on cover, with three quality plastic snap adjustments on each leg and non-wicking binding. These are an excellent, well-designed, no-nonsense cover. WeeBees is also a great source for the Alexis-style nylon pull-on pants, as well as the Bummis Industrial Velcro and snap covers. WeeBees also carries the Aristocrats wool soaker, a super-thick German wool soaker, the Litewrap and the beautiful and well-designed Swedish Bumpy wool Velcro cover by Imse-Vimse. Soon to be introduced is the WeeBees innovative, "convertible" diaper/cover combination, which allows you to snap in extra diaper layers or sizes (including optional snap-in stay-dry liner) as needed into a strong waterproof cover, making an all-in-one if desired. Easy-take-apart components make for thorough washing and drying and they are made of the softest, finest terry velour available.

Rhonda Wiebe has also designed and created "The World's Best Diaper Bag"—and after six children and many inferior diaper bags, I can tell you that this one really makes sense. This is one of the best diaper bags I have ever seen. The World's Best Diaper Bag is made of a hefty, completely machine washable, super-strong 1000 denier Cordura nylon (like a good backpack) and comes in seven solid colors—black (goes well with all my musical instrument bags), navy, purple, gray, forest, sky blue, or cranberry. While other bags may talk about having pockets, this one really does—lined up inside the main compartment, and on the outside, so you can find your Desitin or wipes easily and not have to fumble around the bottom of the bag to look for them (and spill half the contents out trying). Plus, she includes at no extra charge a "little tripper" waist pack, which alone can cost twenty bucks if purchased separately. Plus, you can convert the whole thing to a backpack with two attachable shoulder straps. This bag will last through anything and you will never have to even think of buying one of those cheesy-looking vinyl bags at you-know-where! Don't even think about it! The World's Best Diaper Bag is not at all like the cheap, tacky kinds that wear out after two or three months and leave you having to buy another. Believe me, you don't want to waste your time or money on those! And I am not alone in my assessment—The World's Best Diaper Bag from WeeBees was rated "Best Overall Bag" by the prestigious *Wall Street Journal*!

Diapering accessories offered by WeeBees include Boudreaux's Butt Paste (yes, that's the name), which contains Peruvian Balsam and other skin-healing ingredients; 25 quart and 40 quart round diaper buckets; cloth wipes; industrial strength diaper pins (Rhonda's a devoted pinner); the Snappi; biodegradable diaper liners (which you can reuse if they aren't soiled—including the soft and lovely rice paper liners); nylon ditty bags; the DeoDisks; the two-in-one toilet seat (which you keep on your toilet in lieu of a potty); potty training books; split crotch training pants; hemp layettewear; beautiful, lavender-scented California Baby Botanical Shampoo and Body Wash; and the wipe warmer. Rhonda is also exclusive U.S. distributor of the Little Squirt Water Spray—like a mini power-washer for your diapers that attaches to the plumbing beneath your toilet. Other interesting items include unpetroleum jelly; an herbal salve with goldenseal, calendula, yellow dock, and balm of Gilead (!); the gorgeously-scented line of Burt's Bees products made with honey; The Country Comfort line of herbal baby products (powder, oil, cream); Lansinoh lanolin nipple ointment; natural menstrual products; Kangaroo bibs; natural menstrual products; Baby Wrap baby carrier; wool nursing pads; Medela breast pumps and replacement parts; lambskins; 100-percent-pure lambswool changing/cradle/mattress pads; and wool and diaper washing agents. Gift certificates available.

Mompreneur Rhonda Wiebe says, *"Our business was founded in 1991 to fill a huge hole in the cloth diapering market. Most products we tried were quite awful, but a few shone as wondefully simple, easy and affordable. We have made a conscious decision not to sell anything we would not use ourselves. Most new products seem to lack the functionality and simplicity that we have found to be essential—newfangled, fancy or cute, things that end up in a bin for Goodwill or pawned off on the Internet in a few months. We have been doing cloth diapers for eighteen years; we know what we're doing simply because we've actually done it! From Rhonda and Gary and sons Sean, Ryan, Colin, Ian, Dillon, Kevin and baby Lauren who lives with God!"*

Samples of all diapers available.

Diaper service diapers: Chinese white or unbleached—preemie $2 \times 6 \times 2$ $12 per dozen. Newborn $4 \times 8 \times 4$ $18 per dozen. Regular $4 \times 6 \times 4$ $22 per dozen. Regular $4 \times 8 \times 4$ $25 per dozen. Toddler $4 \times 8 \times 4$ $31 per dozen. European white $4 \times 6 \times 4$ $16.80 per dozen. Regular $4 \times 6 \times 4$ $22 per dozen. Regular $4 \times 8 \times 4$ $25 per dozen. Toddler $4 \times 8 \times 4$ $31 per dozen. **Australian nappy:** $40 per dozen. **Adjustable Snap Cover:** $8.25 each. Sizes to 70 pounds available. **Alexis:** pull-on cover 2-pack $8.50–9. **Aristocrats:** wool soaker $19–25. **Bumpy:** wool velcro cover $19.99 each. **German wool soaker:** $18.50–23.00 each. **Litewrap:** preemie and newborn styles $5.70–6.65 each. **Bummis:** Super whisper Industrial wrap $8.50–9.25 each. Snap wrap $9 each. Shipping based on weight, not price of items ordered.

Product Index

151

DIAPER CHANGES

Product Index

Baby Wipes (reusable)
Pretty much every company selling cloth diapers sells one or more kinds of wipe, washie, what have you. Check the Resource Guide listings under the companies you are looking into. Not all offerings are listed.

Bed Pads

Changing Pads

DeoDisk Diaper Pail Deodorizer

Detergents (natural/ alternative/wool washes)

Diaper Bags

Diaper Buckets (Pails)

Diaper Doublers
Pretty much every company sells some kind of diaper doubler. Check Resource listings or the catalogs themselves for diaper doublers.

Diaper Duck

Diaper Pail Liners (reusable)

Ditty Bags
Pretty much every company sells a form of washable nylon ditty bag. Check with the company you are interested in ordering from.

Diaper Liners (throwaway)

Diaper Liners (reusable)

Gel-Free Disposables

Little Squirt Water Spray

Pins/clips

Pottys/Toilet Seats

Snappi Diaper Fastener

DIAPER CHANGES

Swim Diapers

Training/Bedwetting Pants

Wipe Warmer

154

Appendix A

Adult and Youth Diapering Products

It is my pleasure to make these reusable diapering products known to you. I have used paper products for menstruation, after childbirth, and my own light incontinence problem and I never would again. Cloth products are softer, gentler on sensitive tissues and so much cheaper than paper products in the long run!

Of course, depending on your own need or that of your family member, you might need to use paper products part of the time. You will find here an extensive list of suppliers of comfortable cloth products which you can use as you wish.

The purpose of this listing is to provide legitimately incontinent people with resources to meet their needs. After writing the first edition of this book I was to find out that some people use adult diapering products bizarre fetishes. By providing these resource listings let it be known that I am not endorsing these practices in any way, nor do I encourage the use of this book as a resource for this type of behavior.

I have omitted pricing on these listings because it is rather involved and would depend greatly on your own individual situation. Simply order catalogs or information from the companies of your choosing and talk to their representatives about the costs for your own needs. Although you may spend a considerable amount up front on reusable products, over time you will save money. Just think of the cost of paper products month by month!

May these resources help you and your family to live happier and more comfortably.

Duraline Medical Products
324 Werner Street, P.O. Box 67
Leipsic, OH 45856-1039
800.654.3376

A specialist in incontinent care products. Child diapers to 45 lbs., Velcro youth brief 21" × 33", protective girls' panties and boys' underpants sizes 4-8, Velcro child "easy-access" brief sizes 4 to 8, diaper inserts for children and adults. Diapers include flannel contour adult briefs (waist 21" to 44"), adult Velcro briefs (waist 28" to 54"), adult easy-access pant (waist 22" to 48"), reusable shields (for light dribbling), reusable liners. Covers include adult mesh stretch pant, adult washable cotton pants, child and adult nylon pull-ons (Child's X-small to X-large, Adult X-small to X-large), as well as fashion panty for women and fitted pant for men.

Other important products include reusable underpads for mattresses, enuretic alarm, perineal/ostomy spray cleanser, medicated creams and ointments, body powder, disinfecting sprays and odor eliminators, catheters, drainage bags, gloves, and a slew of disposable products.

Plain packaging available upon request. Medicaid accepted in certain states.

The Windsor Group
P.O. Box 6567
Carlstadt, NJ 07072
800.882.0085

Adult diapering products. For light incontinence, men's brief and boxer shorts, sizes S to 3XL. Ladies panty hip sizes 36 to 46. For moderate to heavy bowel/bladder problems, Ultra-fit brief with snaps Medium to X-Large, Adult diapers regular and large sizes, vinyl waterproof pant S to XL. Washable pads also available.

Windsor Group also carries a slew of Attends disposable products and skin care products such as Peri-wash cleanser, Sween cream, Peri-care creams, Fordustin powder, and odor eliminating spray.

Angel Fluff Diaper Company
P.O. Box 1131
Lewisburg, TN 37091
800.996.2644
customerservice@angelfluff.com
www.angelfluff.com

A specialist in adult and youth incontinence products. Offers soft, well-stitched, all-cotton white flannel diapers in standard, medium, heavy, and extra heavy weights (which they consider possibly the heaviest diaper made). Also offer "The Ultimate Diaper"— a custom-made contour or fitted diaper made to your exact specification with a pattern number assigned just to you. Diaper inserts also available which double diaper absorbency. Unique to Angel Fluff is the "Concealer"— a one-piece snap crotch 100% cotton t-shirt (like babies have), which works well to hide the diapering garments under clothing. Vinyl pull-on and snap overpants in regular and heavyweight styles waist 16" to 60". White, prints, and colors available in polyurethane. Professional Overpant offered in quiet nylon-covered vinyl. Custom pants can be made to your specifications. 54 quart diaper pail, vulcanized flannel bed liners, pillowcases, and large diaper pins (3") also available. All items shipped in plain packaging for your privacy, and your name is not given out to any mailing list.

Baby Love Products
5015-46th St.
Camrose, Alberta T4V 3G3
780.672.1763

Offers bed pads and chair pads. All-in-ones sizes 4-10. Fitted flannel diapers size 4-adult. Padded adult underwear 25" to 50". Adult pants S to L in light, medium, and heavyweight styles. Diapers waist size 25" to 37" and adult all-in-ones 25" to 48".

B.Coole Designs
2631 Piner Rd.
Santa Rosa CA 95401
bc@bcoole.com
www.bcoole.com

Custom-makes diapers in any size and thickness you desire.

WeeBees
3100 S Sheridan Blvd Unit 1C PMB 200.
Denver CO 80227
877-WEE BEES
info@weebees.com
www.weebees.com

Carries WeeBees Adjustable Snap Cover in sizes 32 to 70 lbs. Duratex pull-on coveys in youth and adult sizes X-small to X-large.

Mother-ease
6391 Walmore Road
Niagara Falls, NY 14304
800.416.1475

Mother-ease offers bed wetter pants 30 to 65 lbs All-in-ones to 45 lbs. Toddle-ease diapers 35 to 45 lbs.

DIAPER CHANGES

Babyworks
11725 N.W. West Road
Portland, Oregon 97229
800.645.4349

Carries the excellent Nikky brand training pants to 41 lbs. Nikky nighttime pants 25 to 65 lbs. These have an all-cotton center padding and can hold up to 1 cup of urine. Aristocrats wool soaker to 50 lbs. Bumkins all-in-ones to 42+ lbs.

Aristocrats Baby Products
Box 120
Burton, B.C. V0G 1EO CANADA
250.269.7343
aristo@columbiacable.net

Large child sizes of their 100% wool soakers.

Born to Love
44 Centre Street South
Oshawa, Ontario L1H4C1
905.725.2559

Offers a selection of youth diapering andincontinence products 30 to 50 lbs.

Barefoot Baby
P.O. Box 305
Lewis Center, OH 43035
cservice@barefootbaby.com
www.barefootbaby.com

Bumkins all-in-ones in Junior sizes to 45 lbs. Aristocrats soakers to 50 lbs.

Ecobaby Organics
9319 Northview Terrace
Santee, CA 92071
800.596.7450
www.ecobaby.com

Offers the Aristocrats 100% wool mother-made pull-on soakers in sizes 50 to 70 lbs.

Appendix B

Diaper Pattern and Fabric Sources

Sew Baby
P.O. Box 721
Savoy, IL 61874
800.249.1907
sewbaby@sewbaby.com
www.sewbaby.com

A wonderful catalog and easy-to-use website full of children's patterns, including the Snap Happy Velcro diaper cover. Sells Ultrex in 11 colors,several kinds of seam binding, the Seam Sealer, and silver snaps for making diaper covers.

Interesting patterns include car seat/stroller cover, Kiddy Caddy car tote, baby wrap, complete nursery decor, bags of every size, nursing clothes, shower gifts, fleece outerwear, embroidery,crescent-shaped baby pillow, baby carrier, sleeve-saver bib, Velcro paper dolls, and tote bag barn with 10 stuffed animals to go inside!

The children's patterns include dresses, pinafores, bloomers, hats, sleepwear, layette, raingear, multi-pattern books and playwear, all of boutique quality! Loads of fabrics and notions available. Buy 5 patterns or pattern books and get one free!

Ultrex 58" 8.99 yard (will make 4 to 6 covers per yard!) Seam Sealer $4.95.

Born to Love
15 Silas Hill Dr.
N. York, Ontario, M2J 2X8
416.499.8309

Offers several patterns for diaper products. Snappy Happy is a flannel Velcro diaper 3 sizes. Down Under soaker pattern for knitting your own wool soakers in a cute tie-on style! All sizes, $2.49. Back to Basic Diaper Patterns offers 5 diaper styles, 3 diaper cover styles, and numerous variations— from flat diaper to old English terry nappy to heavy-duty prefold, to an all-in-one and more. Elizabeth Lee nursing clothes patterns are gorgeous and easy to make, ranging from dresses to blouses to bathing suits to nightgowns and more. Make those designer nursing clothes for less! Some children's clothes and bibs patterns also offered, including the Easy Sewing line of basic patterns for infants, children, and adults. Remember 30% lower prices due to exchange rate.

Baby Love Products/Kidalog
5015-46 St.
Camrose, Alberta T4V 3G3
780.672.6942
www.kidalog.com

Offers the very good Baby Softwear fitted diaper pattern which is sleek and designed to fit well under the Nikky line of diaper covers, $5.95. Also offers a special sewing kit of precut diapers, elastic, sample diaper and instructions in regular and organic fabrics. Waterproof nylon, 60", bleachable elastic, and unbleached, organic cotton, 59".

Amazon Dry Goods
2218 E. 11th Street
Davenport, IA 52803-3760
800.798-7979

Sells 36" birdseye $2.75 yard. Quick-Sew pattern to make Velcro fitted diapers and diaper covers. (If using Ultrex for covers, just use that; omit outer cotton layer).

Pattern catalog features 1,100 patterns from medieval through 19th century $7.00, General catalog carries every conceivable type of 19th century merchandise, $4.00. Shoe catalog has 158 styles of historic reproductions from all periods, children's to adults, $5.00. Window Treatment Catalog, $3.00

Ecobaby Organics
332 Coogan Way
El Cajon, CA 92020
888. ECO.BABY
ginny@ecobaby.com
www.ecobaby.com

Offers a generous supply of organic cotton fabric, including flannel, chambray, jersey, and tube rib. Also offers untreated Ecospun knit made from recycled soda bottles in a variety of solid colors. Changeable inventory— call for what's available.

B.Coole Designs
2631 Piner Rd.
Santa Rosa CA 95401
bc@bcoole.com
www.bcoole.com

Sells 36" diaper fabric $4.00/yard which can be dyed in light, low-impact dye colors.

www.diapersewing.com

Check out this website for diaper and cover sewing tips and links to patterns, fabric and notions.

Appendix C

Diapering Websites and Further Info

If the information and company/product reviews I have provided in Diaper Changes has not quenched your thirst for diapering knowledge, I have provided links and reviews of a few good websites for your perusal (there certainly are plenty others). Please be aware that some chat rooms/message boards have become very petty and small-minded about every stupid little thing in diaper-world, and do not reflect the spirit in which I wrote this book. Please also be very, very aware that if you do a search for diapers or diapering on the internet (particuarly those with adult incontinence needs) you may come across websites dealing with adult diaper fetishes (don't ask). Please be careful what you are getting into; the sites I have visited and listed below as of this writing are good and safe.

clothdiaperinginfo.org
Lots of diapering information, company and product ratings with consumer input, diaper swap, and bookstore (selling this book!).

diapers.net
Good no-frills site with lists of merchants and sites dealing with cloth diapering.

kindercloset.com
An internet consignment shop where you can find and sell used diapering products as well as children's and adult clothing and much more.

boards.parentsplace.com
Has a well-traveled diapering message board. Don't spend all your time on the site (as some seem to do) or your world will get very small and out of focus!

diapersewing.com
I wish this site existed when I was sewing diapers! Offers sewing tips for diapers and covers and sources for diaper and cover fabric and notions. It links to:

Diapering Websites and Further Info

diaperpin.com
A site offering product/company reviews (every new company that popped up this week), and used diapering products for sale/trade.

realnappy.com
A British website dealing with diapering issues related to cloth diapering in Europe.

borntolove.com
Self-proclaimed "diapering Mecca" website from Canada with many merchant advertisers, product and company reviews, message board, and consumer input.

wen.org.uk
The website for the Women's Environmental Network, which has a large grassroots movement in Britain advocating cloth diapers and other issues related to women and child heatlh and the environment.

diapernet.com
The website for the National Association of Diaper Services (NADS).

Appendix D

Research Sources

The following articles, studies, booklets, leaflets, pamphlets, promotional materials, books, and persons were consulted in the preparation for the Costs of Diapering, the Environmental Realities of Diapering, The Health and Safety of Diapering, and other portions of *Diaper Changes*:

Acohido, Byron. "Baby Diapers Emerging as a Market in Ontario." *Waste News*, 3/25/96.

Armstrong, Liz, and Scott, Adrienne. *Whitewash: Exposing the dangers of women's sanitary products and disposable diapers— what you can do about it.* Toronto: Harper Perennial, 1992.

Bayles, Fred. "The Diaper Dilemma." *Santa Rosa Press Democrat*, 7/3/89, D1&D2.

Baudry, Ann. "Biodegradable Diapers: A Pseudo Solution." *Mothering*, Fall 1989, p.32-33.

Becker, Ellen. "Are Single-Use Diapers Compostable?" *Mothering*, Summer 1991, p.53.

Center For Policy Alternatives, *Update on Diapers*, Washington, 9/90.

Christensen, Jackie Hunt. Women's Environmental Network. Personal Communication, Spring and Fall 1996.

Cooper, Joan. "Cloth or Disposables— Give Common Sense A Chance!" Executive Vice-President of Biobottoms, Inc. Informational material, 9/10/94.

Cornell Cooperative Extension. Informational Diapering Brochure, New York, 1990.

Cummings, Joy Towles. President, Help Our Polluted Environment (HOPE), Taylor County, Florida. Personal Communication. Spring 1996.

—"Reach for the Unbleached— The Campaign for Chlorine-Free Papers." *HOPE for Taylor County Newsletter*, 3/25/96, p.14.

—"HOPE to Plug P&G/Buckeye Mill's Discharge Plant." *HOPE for Taylor County Newsletter*, 3/25/96, p.1.

Dadd, Debra Lynn. *Nontoxic, Natural, and Earthwise.* New York: G.P. Putnam's Sons, 1990.

De Jong, Greta Belanger. "Disposable Diapers." *Catalyst*, Feb/March 1989.

Electric Power Research Institute. 1995 figures as reported by General Public Utilities System, Fall 1996.

Garlington, JoAnn. "Toss Aways Easy on Moms." *Santa Rosa Press Democrat*, 7/3/89.

General Diaper Service, Piscataway, NJ. "The Diaper Report: The Results Are In." Informational Brochure, Received Fall 1996.

Hollis, Robert.

— "The Diaper Wars." *Mothering*, Summer 1991, p.48.

— "The Ethics of Diapering." *Mothering*, Fall 1898, p.29.

Hughes, Vivien Santana. "Diapers." *LA Parent Magazine*, 1/92, P. 24, 68.

Research Sources

Johnson, Lorraine. "Study-Slinging." *Earthkeeper* (Guleph, Ontario) reprint., p.14-17.

King County Nurses Association, Seattle, Washington.

— Health Issue Position Paper: Health and Environmental Issues Related to Disposable Diapers. 1992.

— "Diapering Baby: What's the Bottom Line?" Brochure produced in conjunction with King County Solid Waste Division, Seattle, Washington. Received Spring 1996.

Knowlton, Ken. President, Baby's Dy-Dee Service, Lancaster, Pennsylvania. Personal Communication, Fall 1996.

Krushel, Sharon. Coordinator, Peace River Childbirth Education Association "Alternatives in Diapering" Educational Booklet), Peace River, Alberta, Personal Communication, Spring 1996.

La Croix, Susan. "Diapers: Getting to the Bottom of Things." *Mothering*, Summer 1993, p. 41.

Lehrburger, Carl. Personal Communication, Spring and Fall, 1996.

Lust, John. *The Herb Book*. New York: Bantam Books, 1974.

Lyman, Francesca, "Diaper Hype." *Garbage*, Jan/Feb 1990, p.38.

Mazar, Ann S. "The Disposable Diaper Dilemma." *E Magazine*, May/June 1990.

Mautz, Kathy. Former Executive Director, National Association of Diaper Services. Personal Communication, Spring 1996.

Mothering Staff, "The Dioxin Connection." *Mothering*, Fall 1989.

National Association of Diaper Services. Informational/ promotional sheets, 1995.

New York State Consumer Protection Board. "Cloth or Disposable Diapers: The Consumer's Choice." Informational Brochure received Fall 1996.

Office of Waste Reduction Services, State of Michigan, Departments of Commerce and Natural Resources. Case Study, Gretchen's House III Child Care, Ann Arbor, Michigan. February 1992.

Primomo, Janet, PhD, RN. Assistant Professor, University of Washington-Tacoma School of Nursing. Personal Communication, Spring 1996.

—"The High Environmental Cost of Disposable Diapers." (Primomo, et. al). *Maternal-Child Health*, September/ October 1990, p. 279-284.

—Influencing Policy on Diapering: Not for Babies Only." (Primomo and Greenstreet, Patricia, JD, RN). *Journal of Perinatology*, vol. XIII, no. 2, 1993, p. 140-143.

Proctor and Gamble.

— "A Closer Look At Disposables." Informational Brochure, 1995.

— In conversation with their spokesperson, Spring and Fall 1996.

Poore, Patricia. "Disposable Diapers: They're OK, You're OK." Garbage, Oct/Nov 1992, p.28-31.

Peace River Childbirth Education Association, "Alternatives in Diapering." Educational Booklet. Peace River, Alberta, 1995.

Rathje, William and Murphy, Cullen. "Cotton vs. Disposables: What's the Damage?" *Garbage*, Oct/Nov 1992, p.29.

Scott, Adrienne. Co-author, *Whitewash*. Personal Communication, Summer 1996.

Shiffert, Jack. National Association of Diaper Services. Personal Communication, Fall 1996.

DIAPER CHANGES

Sinclair, Lani, "EPA Reconsiders Dioxins, Again." *Safety and Health*, 2/95., p.79-80.

Smolonsky, Marc. "Dioxin in Single-Use Diapers and Tampons." *Mothering*, Summer 1993, p.45-48.

Swasy, Alecia. *Soap Opera: The Inside Story of Proctor & Gamble*. New York: Times Books (Random House), 1993.

Thompson-Shore, Inc. "Chlorine-Free Paper...What's It All About." *Printer's Ink*, vol 12, issue 1, p.2.

Tibbals, Sue., et. al. "WEN: Towards Truth in Environmental Marketing." *Mothering*, Summer 1993, p.40.

U.S. Consumer Product Safety Commission, National Injury Information Clearinghouse.

—Report on Disposable Diapers, Reported Incidents, 1994 to 10/22/96.

—Report on Cloth Diapers, Reported Incidents and Accident Investigations, 1/80 to 10/96.

Vermont Agency of Natural Resources, Recycling and Resource Conservation Section. "Diapers: Cloth versus Disposables: It's Your Choice". Informational Pamphlet received in 1996.

The following resources may also be of interest:

Franklin Associates, Ltd. "Energy and Environmental Profile Analysis of Children's Cloth and Disposable Diapers." Prairie Village, Kansas, July 1990. (Report to the American Paper Institute)

Lehrburger, Carl, et. al. "Diapers: Environmental Impacts and Lifecycle Analysis." January 1991 (Report to the National Association of Diaper Services)

Lentz, Little. "Environmental Profile of Cloth and Disposable Diapering Systems." June 1989 (Proctor & Gamble Employee)

Little, Arthur D., Inc. "Disposable versus Resusable Diapers." Cambridge, Massachusetts, March 1990 (Report to Proctor & Gamble)

Society of Environmental Toxicology and Chemistry (SETAC).

—"A Technical Framework for Lifecycle Assessment". January 1991.

—"Environmental Assessment of Products." Report of a Consultation. January 1992-October 1993.

Women's Environmental Network. "Memorandum to the Advertising Standards Authority from the Women's Environmental Network: Pampers and the Environment." London: July, 1991.

The following are studies on diaper rash:

Austin, et. al. "A Survey of Factors Associated with Diaper Dermatitis in 36 Pediatric Practices." *J. Pediatric Health Care 2*, 295-299, 1988.

Campbell, R.L., et. al. "Clinical Studies with Disposable Diapers Containing Absorbent Gelling Material." *J. American Academy of Dermatology*, 17:978-989, 1987.

Jordan, W.E., et.al. "Diaper Dermatitis: Frequency and Severity Among a General Infant Population." *Pediatric Dermatology* 1986;3(3); 198-207.

Keller, Phillip E. "Diaper Dermatitis". *Canada Family Physician* 36:1569-1572, 1990.

Seymour, Jon. L., et. al. "Clinical Effects of Diaper Types." *American Academy of Dermatology*, 17: 988-997, 1987.

Research Sources

The following data were used to provide statistics for the Costs of Diapering (costs do not include taxes, shipping charges except where noted, or any other variable not specified):

All figures are based on an average of 70 changes per week for 130 weeks.

HOME DIAPERING:

#1 Diapers: costs per dozen (examples)

shaped 41.00
flannel terry 20.00
birdseye prefold 20.00
plushie prefold 37.00
Mother's choice 29.00
Velcro diapers 20-60.00
double duty 50.00
gn cotton terry prefold 32.00
plushie contour 38.00
terry prefold gn cot 30.00
Chinese d.s. prefold 25.00
gn cotton gauze 30.00
Sandy's 108.00
Popolino 102.00

#2 Diaper cover prices (examples)

Biobottoms wool covers
5 small & medium 170.00+
5 medium, large, xlg 262.50-432.50

Nikky cotton
25 covers 362.50

Wool pull-on soaker
25 covers 402.50

Nat Baby Velcro
cheap nylon Velcro.
25 covers 79.00

Nat Baby nylon pull-ons
25 covers 91.25

Polyester Nikkys
25 covers 275.00

Alexis snap nylon pull-ons
25 covers 97.00

Bummis
nylon pants Velcro 91.25

Nikky wool
25 covers 462.50

Diaperaps
25 covers 150.00

Bumkins (all-in-ones)
5 doz. at 10.00 600.00
(no additional diapers to buy)

#3 Detergents

Tide, at 18¢ load, 2 loads/wk, 130 wks=$46.80
Ivory Snow, at 26¢ load, 2 loads/wk, 130 wks=$67.60
Borax at 12¢ load, 2 loads/wk, 130 wks=$31.20

Tide/Borax Combo, per load= 30c
Ivory Snow/Borax Combo, per load= 38c

Average of Tide/Borax and Snow/Borax combos, per load= 34c
Average of Tide/Borax and Ivory Snow/Borax combinations, 2 loads/week, 130 weeks= 88.40

#4 Electricity

Rates based on National Electric Power Research Institute's National Averages, 1995.

One load: wash, 19 cents (hot/cold) dry, 40 cents (one hour hot).
Weekly cost (2 loads/wk): 1.18
Yearly cost: 61.36
Total diapering period cost:
(130 weeks, 2 loads/week)=153.40

DIAPER SERVICE:

The costs for diaper service were based on discussion with the National Association of Diaper Services, Fall 1996.

DIAPER CHANGES

The $275.00 average cost for diaper covers is the average of the low-end and high-end diaper covers ($100-450.00). This averages out to 3 cents per change additional for 9, 100 changes (70 per week for 130 weeks).

DISPOSABLES:

The costs for disposables were based on the national average price for Pampers, March 1996, as reported by Proctor & Gamble spokesperson, Fall 1996.

National average price= $6.92 per bag (all sizes);.24 each
size 1= 40 diapers per bag, .17 each
size 2= 34 " .20 "
size 3= 28 " .25 "
size 4= 24 " .29 "
size 5= 22 " .31 "

Prices for rural Pennsylvania were based on a mean average of the following prices in Myerstown Pennsylvania, Fall 1995:

The cost for suburban Californian disposable price was based on conversation with suburban L.A. parent, Fall 1995.

A 2 cent garbage disposal cost per disposable was based on statistics provided by the Vermont Agency of Natural Resources, Recycling and Resource Conservation Section (see reference above).

Please also consult the "Alternatives in Diapering" booklet listed in the sources above for a super-scientific analysis of diapering costs, including specific drying times of various diaper types.

Pampers
newborn . . . . .15¢
small/medium . . . . .19¢
medium . . . . 21¢
large . . . . .19¢

Cuddles
no small size
medium . . . . 19¢
large . . . . .24¢
extra large . . . . .14¢

Shur-Fine
no newborn size
medium . . . . 18¢
large . . . . .25¢
thins large . . . . .24¢
medium thin . . . . .18¢

Drypers
no small size
medium . . . . 18¢
large . . . . .24¢
extra large . . . . .27¢

Fitti
Same as Shur-Fine.

Huggies
Same as Pampers.

Luvs
small . . . . .12¢
medium . . . . .15¢
large . . . . .23¢
extra large . . . . .25¢

Wal-Mart
small . . . . .12¢

"ALTERNATIVE" Disposable
(Tushies, club price, including shipping):
Average price= $42.95/case;33 cents each
Premature/newborn= 270 diapers/case, 16 cents each

small= 160 . . . . .27¢ "
medium= 120 . . . . .36¢ "
large= 88 . . . . .49¢ "
toddler= 80 . . . . .54¢ "

168

Now That You Are Done

A Note from the Author to You

My sincerest thanks to all my readers. It has been a pleasure to think of you as a variety of mothers, babies, and families as I wrote *Diaper Changes*, knowing this will be a tool you can use in your busy, fruitful lives. It is a labor of love, from my heart to yours.

Above all
I encourage mothers in particular, to love your children. Enjoy them. Relish the time with them. Have fun and laugh and feel and live side by side with them. With a thankful and grateful heart, the matters of diapering (or any other duty), though not entirely pleasant, become rich fulfillments in the life and call of motherhood.

May your children grow to find all the best of what truly matters in life, and may you help them there.

Acknowledgments

I wish to thank the following people who have helped me in various ways during the conception, writing, and publishing of *Diaper Changes:*

Eileen Pereira Arndt, for over 30 years of friendship, the hours spent computerizing the manuscript of the first edition (not realizing what she was getting into!), and her generous, gracious spirit.

Bernice Bestwina, for her marvelous dry diaper method, straight from the heart of Brooklyn.

Kathy Mautz and Jack Shiffert of the National Association of Diaper Services, for their assistance, and the gracious use of the diaper illustration idea in Chapter 5.

Jackie Hunt Christensen of the Women's Environmental Network, for her helpful scrutiny of the book's environmental and health information, with particular attention to dioxin-related matters.

Carl Lehrburger, for his unique perspective on solid waste issues.

Adrienne Scott, co-author of *Whitewash*, whose logical and helpful suggestions helped clear much befuddlement.

Liz Moses of the Washington Toxics Coalition, for her critical review of the health and environmental material, and insightful editorial comments.

Bob Herd, of General Health Care Corporation, for his practical suggestions and support.

Carolyn Dash Mailler of *Parenting From The Heart* magazine, who started me on the road to writing for other parents.

Philip Weaver, for excellent design work on the self-published editions and willingness to undertake this project with the uniquenesses involved.

Katy Jay, who did a great proof-reading job on the first edition.

Susette Jurek, for the soakers-from-old-sweaters idea.

Rhonda Wiebe and her son Sean, for a magnificent job producing my website, and especially to Rhonda for all her advice, support, prayers, and encouragement.

Rik Lain Schell, for going with serendipidity and creating this trade edition.

The owners and manufacturers and distributors of diapering products reviewed in this book, who have allowed me to sample their prod-

170

Acknowledgments

ucts for review, for their excitement about and encouragement throughout my writing *Diaper Changes*.

The many, many moms who have taken the time to write and express how they feel about *Diaper Changes*. This has touched my heart and given me vision when the focus gets blurry. I thank you all for your kind, encouraging words.

The Alpha and Omega, the beginning and the end of this project, thanks, praise and glory.

About the Author

Vida Theresa Rodriguez Farrisi was born in Manhattan and spent most of her life in and around New York City. In addition to being an award-winning author, Theresa is a professional singer and is currently completing her Master of Music degree in voice pedagogy and performance at Westminster Choir College. She teaches voice privately in addition to singing, choir conducting, and working in church music.

Diaper Changes was a 1998 Writer's Digest *National Self-Published Book Award* winner and has appeared in other books such as *The Consumer Reports Guide to Baby and Children's Products*, *The Mothers and Others Guide to Natural Baby and Child Care*, *Baby Bargains*, Carla Emery's *Encyclopedia of Country Living*, and *Attachment Parenting*. Theresa's work has appeared in parenting magazines such as *Mothering, Pregnancy, Parenting From The Heart* and *The Wise Mother*. Theresa is also author of *When Adoption Fails* and is working on a new book entitled "Practical Parenting."

Theresa is the joyful mother of six cloth-diapered, exclusively breastfed and attachment-parented children: Francesca, Angelica, Anthony, Gloria, Gabriella, and Sophia, and currently makes her home in Pennsylvania Dutch Country.

INDEX